Lost to Found
IN 90 DAYS

Written By:

Rachel Adams & Nina Rowan Heller

Publication Notice

Copyright Notice

All materials are © 2015 Lost to Found, LLC. All rights reserved.

No part of this publication and its associated materials may be reproduced or transmitted in any form or by any means without the prior permission of the authors.

Disclaimer: The advice and workbook exercises contained herein may not be suitable for every situation. This book is not intended as a substitute for the medical advice of physicians. The reader should regularly consult a physician in matters relating to his/her health. The author has made every effort to ensure the accuracy of the information within this book was correct at time of publication. The author does not assume and hereby disclaims any liability to any party for any loss, damage, or disruption caused by errors or omissions, whether such errors or omissions result from accident, negligence, or any other cause.

Cover Illustration & Design Copyright © 2015 Mustard Square, LLC
Editing by Pamela Saez, Jonathan Moerbe, & Ryan Lee
Authors photographs by Octavio Valencia

Contents

Lost to Found Background

About the Authors.. 1
Dedication.. 3
Gratitude... 4

Chapters

1. Your Story and Your "Big Why"................................. 11
2. Your Two Distractions.. 28
3. Your Day: Planning and Implementing.......................... 42
4. Your Water.. 60
5. Your Nutrition and Fuel...................................... 70
6. Your Exercise and Sleep...................................... 83
7. Your Mindset and Body Posture................................ 100
8. Your Journal... 120
9. Your Relationship Standards and Allies....................... 133
10. Your Goals and Lists.. 146
11. Your Spirituality and Meditation............................ 158
12. Your Quiet Time and Self-Love............................... 173

Final Note to the Reader 185

About the Authors

Rachel Adams

Rachel Adams is the co-founder of Aitchison and Adams Real Estate team at Keller Williams Realty. She is currently ranked in the top 1% of all Realtors in Placer and Sacramento counties. Her team is anticipated to close nearly $50 million in sales for the year 2016. Last year, she was named to "The Wall Street Journal's Top 1,000 Agents" in the United States.

When not actively selling homes, Rachel can be found traveling the U.S. with her business partner, coaching others on how to build a successful real estate team with a winning mindset. She has a love for public speaking and enjoys seeing the positive effect her experience brings to the lives of others. While real estate is in her blood, her greatest joy comes from encouraging others to lead their best lives.

Rachel's love for inspiring others, combined with her own unique and powerful journey, led her to create the Lost to Found 90 Day Program. This empowering program leads people to live their best lives. With her large and successful presence on Facebook and other social media platforms, she is excited to share this with people around the world, and is poised to create a global network of "Lost to Founders" who are committed to living lives of intention, great success, and well-being.

Rachel lives in Folsom, California with her boyfriend Ryan. They lead an active life and love all things outdoors. Rachel loves to blast great music while creating healthy meals in their newly renovated kitchen. She also loves to travel, participate in growth seminars, and serve as an ambassador for a local anti-sex-trafficking non-profit. If you've had the pleasure of spending time in Rachel's presence, you know that she loves deep conversations that end with a hug! She is passionate about living life to the fullest, and chooses happiness above all else.

Nina Rowan Heller

Nina Rowan Heller founded Rowan Health Concepts in 1994 because of her passion for health and fitness. Her background as a mental health professional and drive for solutions create a unique, comprehensive approach for clients in Austin, San Diego, around the country, and around the world.

Nina assists clients with finding the inspiration and tools they need to create foundations for long term healthy lifestyles. She is an educational and motivational speaker for individuals, small businesses and corporate clients. Nina has seen that creating optimal health for the individuals in a business will improve energy level, productivity and morale of that business.

To accommodate her clients, Nina travels for intensive assessments, consultations and interventions. Most clients experience the power and success of her work through weekly phone sessions. Nina has and continues to serve top executives, leaders, actors, sports figures, and Olympic athletes.

Nina is a very active wife and stepmother of 4 children. She resides in Austin, Texas and San Diego, California. She loves doing anything outdoors, traveling, and meeting new people. Nina loves challenges, believes the body is amazing, and knows that staying curious pushes her to learn and expand every day.

Dedication

This book is dedicated to anyone longing for transformation.
If you've ever closed your eyes and felt stuck…

If you know there is so much more out there
but you don't know how to get it...

Craving change is a powerful force.

Set your intention and we'll provide the momentum
for you to go from
Lost to Found.

Gratitude

There are so many amazing people who played a vital role in making *Lost to Found* a reality.

Without their help, this powerful program and book would still be our best kept secret. Deepest gratitude to our Lost to Found creative team!

Special gratitude from Nina to Rachel...

Sweet Rachel, I knew you were someone special when you entered the room for our first meeting. How so much powerful, magnetic energy could emanate from such a small frame caught my attention. In spite of your petite size there is nothing small about you! In the 20 plus years of working with people, your heart stands out among them. Your immense desire to make sure others have the opportunity to experience the same high level of success you have experienced is commendable. Creating Lost to Found with such a dynamic partner has been quite the journey, especially in light of our busy schedules! Thank you for being the spark, the courage, the tenacity, and the inspiration for creating a program to help so many others reach their highest potential.

Special gratitude from Rachel to Nina...

Loving Nina, thank you for your honesty, your coaching skills, your huge knowledge base, and our powerful friendship. When you asked me to share my story, I was terrified of being that vulnerable. The safe space you offered, encouraged me to go outside my comfort zone and transform my vulnerability into strength and wisdom. What a journey! Knowing this was for the benefit of others has kept me going – in spite of the crazy hours! Thank you for challenging me to find the best version of myself. The time spent at your beach house creating this work, has been one of my most treasured memories. I truly thank you, my sweet friend, for being exactly as you are. I love you!

Our L2F90 Family

Lauren Kelly

Our Project Manager/Designer… aka our lifeline! Thank you so much for riding in on your white horse (with your trusty USB drive) and organizing our multifaceted world. You've kept us sane through all of the unknown craziness that is involved in a project of this size and scope. We couldn't have asked for a better person to do the job!

Pamela Saez

Our Editor - Oh sweet Pam! I don't think we can ever thank you enough for your magical way with words. Finding our voice, when we didn't know how to say what we wanted to say, was a gift. Thank you for guiding our discussions, notes, thoughts, and ideas and into this powerful book and manuscript. This wouldn't be the same without you.

Matt Moores and Mario Colangelo

Our Videographers - We saw that twinkle in your eyes the very first time we sat down to discuss our plans for this project, and we knew you had something special in mind. Your amazing talent for taking our words and turning them into visual magic has floored us. We are so lucky that we got to utilize your talent before your huge movie careers take off! Thank you for your vision and dedication to our program.

Tavio (Top Hat Tavio) Valencia

Our Photographer - We bow to your amazing eye! Thank you for putting us at ease and making us laugh to get the perfect photos. We deeply appreciate the time and care you put into making sure every photo captured the essence of what we were going for.

Jonathan Moerbe

Our Content Strategist - The moon and stars aligned at the perfect moment for you to jump into this project and we're so grateful. We will miss our late night video chats from different time zones. Your sense of humor, even at the eleventh hour, was a complete gift to work with. We are so grateful for your knowledge, guidance, and patience with this book.

Brittani Hill

Our Marketing Rep and Personal Assistant Extraordinaire - Thank you for consistently going above and beyond for this program. You've been right there for every email and text (day or night) and we're humbled. Immense thanks for making our lives flow so smoothly. You are our shining star! Our fellow readers/challengers are lucky to have you as a part of their lives for their 90 day challenge!

Phoebe Verkouw

Our Fashionista Stylist - Thirty one outfit changes in five days! We literally could not have done this without you! Thank you so much for your fashion savvy, your huge heart, and always making sure that our hair and makeup were flawless for every shoot. The difference you made was stellar. Stay tuned for Phoebe's Fashions. Her boutique is sure to be a huge hit and we're so proud of her!

Rachel's Gratitude

Anita Dizon

My Business, turned Life-Coach, turned Family - Oh my sweet love, where do I begin? Not everyone is so lucky to find the kind of friendship that we have found. I met you in a professional capacity but God had so much more in store for us! Thank you for all of the conversations we've had that reached a level of depth I have never known. Thank you for challenging me to dig deeper and find the woman I was meant to be. Our friendship means the world to me. I will always admire you and feel hugely blessed to be able to call you my other mama.

To the Power-Girlfriends...

I started to list all of your names and then it seemed silly. You know who you are! You are the gemstones in my life. THANK YOU! You know me better than I know myself. Thank you for the countless hours shared on your assorted couches under a blanket. Thank you for supporting me in my darkest hours while I rediscovered who I was. Thank you for never giving up on me, and encouraging me to venture beyond the surface. Thank you for your constant love-packed texts and calls. Every photo you've ever sent from random times in our lives are treasured memories. I wouldn't be where I am today without your laughter and support. You are the most amazing bunch of female leaders I could ever ask for and I'm forever grateful.

Matt Aitchison

My Business Partner - 5 years ago when we met at that little real estate office, I could never have imagined the path we would have embarked on together. Thank you for your friendship, your patience and willingness to share in our joint growth process, your continual drive to make us better as a company, your commitment to our team, and mostly your big heart. Even though we fight like brother and sister, I never take for granted that you are one of the most important people in my life! I am so grateful for you.

Dianna Kokoszka

My Biggest Female Mentor! I remember watching your coaching videos during my first BOLD experience as a brand new agent at KW. That was four years ago. I've taken it six times since then! Your programs and coaching have changed our company and made it a first-class environment. My mindset has blossomed because of your teachings and I now want more for myself because you told me I was allowed to dream BIG. Thank you for being the strong woman that you are. You have inspired my life greatly.

Keller Williams Realty

My Amazing Real Estate Company. Some might think it's unusual to have a dedication to your company. However, KW has my deepest respect and holds an important place in my heart. The incredible leadership of Gary, Mark, Mo, Dianna, Mary, and now Chris and John have brought so much wisdom, heart, and experience to so many. When I came to this company years ago, I had no idea how much it would influence me. KW is more than a company; it's a philosophy. Its innovative classes ensure that you reach your true potential. They have expanded my mind, made a huge impact on my success level, and keep me stretching for new horizons. I now have friends all over the world that I refer to as my KW Family.

I love my life, and a huge reason why I do, is because of the people I get to be surrounded by daily in this amazing company. Thank you wholeheartedly.

Don Erik Wolff

Thank you for being such a strong force in my life for so many years. Not many people can say (or would want to) that they moved their best friend 6 times. Lucky you! You always have a joke ready, a humorous message or a big hug to share. What's better than that! You are one of the best people I know and I am so happy you are in my life!

To Rachel's Family...

Mom and Dad, growing up, I always knew that I was lucky. To be raised with the kind of love that you two share -- it's just not something that every kid gets to experience. Thank you for showing me what a healthy relationship is, and providing the blueprint to build one. Not every person grows up fortunate enough to be able to call their parents friends. I get to call you my best friends. Thank you for your many hours on the phone allowing me to bounce ideas off of you for this book. You listened to my journal entries, wiped away countless tears, and supported my process of self-discovery as only you two could. Knowing that I am who I am today because I was your little girl means the world to me. I love you both so much!

Brian and Stu

My Brothers -
Brian, I remember a time when we were inseparable as kids. Though life has presented us with some challenges and a steady flow of change, I know we are still deeply connected. Always praying for you big brother. I love you.

Stuart, thank you for that talk on the beach two years ago on Thanksgiving. It was during that talk that I discovered the elusive, missing piece to my puzzle -- self-love. I know you and I have not always seen eye to eye but I am so proud of the man you are becoming. You have such a big heart and are worthy of the best that love has to offer. I am excited to watch all your dreams come true.

Ryan Lee

Love of My Life - I remember months ago sitting quietly on my couch. I was writing out my list of all the things that I wanted in a partner. I wasn't sure it was even out there. When I met you, I realized my list was standing in front of me. In fact, you well surpassed my list! Now I get to hang out with my best friend every day, and what a giant bonus that I happen to be ridiculously in love with you. Thank you for your endless hours of comfort, warmth, guidance, and support during the creation of this program. You have made me feel like a best-selling author from day one. When I was stressed out, you held me with loving arms. When I was doubting myself, you told me all the things I needed to hear. When I wanted to take a break, you would slow dance with me in the kitchen. You have never stopped showing me how much you believe in me. I feel like you are the biggest gift I could possible receive, for my amazing 90 day journey! Thank you for being one of the most brilliant, kind, funny, affectionate, and caring men that I know. I am so lucky to be loved by you.

Nina's Gratitude

My Clients

To my clients, thank you from the bottom of my heart. You are my true teachers and my chosen family and friends. It has been a privilege to create such long term working relationships with you. Thank you for your trust and for making our work together a priority in your life. It is because of you that I have been able to do something that I love and I hope you know how much you mean to me.

Keller Williams Leadership

I have been so very fortunate to have some of the most talented leaders, mentors, and coaches as my clients. Thank you Gary Keller for sharing your brilliant strategic mind and actually using your white board during our workouts. Thank you for becoming a true friend and for knowing me enough to recognize my soulmate and bring us together. Thank you Dianna Kokozska for blazing the trail for me and so many other women to follow their dreams and make them successful. Your immense intelligence, leadership, innovative design thinking, and perseverance has made it possible for me to do what I love. Thank you Mo Anderson for your dedication and commitment to years of 5:00 a.m. training sessions. I'm grateful for your wisdom, and for showing me what courage really looks like. Thank you Mary Tenant. When I stepped into the complex and demanding role of stepmom for four amazing kids, your wise counsel was absolutely indispensable. My gratitude for how you've helped my family is huge and unending. Your support and understanding is appreciated more than you will ever know.

Chris Heller

My Loving Husband - thank you so much for being the man who understands me on the deepest level. Your constant appreciation, support, and sense of humor make life a wonderful journey. Partnering with such a dynamic force is an adventure I love and treasure, along with the four other loves in my life that you brought me. I am eternally grateful for our family.

To the Kids

Thank you to the kids: Alexandra, Sophia, Nicholas, and Olivia. I loved you the moment I met you and saw your father in each one of you. Thank you for accepting me into your lives and allowing me to love you. Watching and helping you grow has been a privilege. Thank you Alli. Every day I learn by witnessing your strength. Thank you Sophie. Your huge caring heart is an inspiration for all of us. Thank you Nick. Your steady and wise presence in a family filled with strong women is a gift. Thank you Livvy. Your bright mind and curiosity have been a complete pleasure to support. Our full lives are quite the adventure and I love, appreciate and respect all of you and your immense potential.

To My Family

Thank you to my parents, Vern and Kathleen, my siblings, Lisa, Steve, and Lora, and their families. I believe my powerful desire to help others has come from my family. Mom and Dad, you modeled how to care for people, how to do things well, and how to do them with endless stamina. You taught me the importance and value of placing personal relationships as the centerpiece of a good and whole life. I also credit my success to three highly intelligent, brutally honest, incredibly funny siblings. I love you all.

The Bodies We Are Dealt

And finally I would like to thank God for the unique and wonderful vehicle I was given to explore life with. Without my physical challenges I would never have pursued health with quite the same gusto. My back, with its special challenges, caused me to explore a world far beyond western medicine, whose solutions have often been unacceptable, and totally irrelevant. These experiences have been catalysts for finding far better solutions, which have served not only me but my clients well.

And of course, thank you, dear reader, for joining this journey!

Chapter 1:
Your Story and Your "Big Why"

Rachel's Journey

My palms were sweaty with excitement. I was in the height of my career and minutes away from being interviewed on camera about my path to success and how in three short years, my real estate team had gone from 0 transactions to just over 200 homes sold. We were now a leading sales team in our county and had hit the top 1%. This video I was being interviewed for was going to be shown to thousands of agents in the hope of inspiring them.

The location for shooting was in a gym at my company's corporate headquarters in Austin, TX. A woman named Nina Rowan Heller was interviewing me. Nina was the fitness/wellness coach for the top leadership of Keller Williams Realty. One of her clients happened to be my biggest mentor, Dianna Kokoszka. In 2012, I had taken a Keller Williams' coaching course called BOLD that she had designed. This amazing sales course focused greatly on your personal growth as well as business. Not only did it completely shift my mindset and start off my career, it also inspired me to lose 40 pounds. The video was to showcase my routine every morning – it would demonstrate how following a successful morning routine sets the foundation of your day and has directly affected the success of my business.

As the videographer prepared, I waited anxiously for my name to be called with this one antagonizing thought… I was no longer 40 pounds lighter! Life had presented me with a series of challenges over the last few years (divorce, stress, depression, and a frenetic schedule). I had now gained back 30 of those 40 pounds! My days involved long hours of hard work, followed by happy hours, dinner with friends, and sometimes late night drinks at a third venue.

Rinse and Repeat

You've heard the expression, "rinse and repeat"? This had now taken on a whole new meaning for me that had my body struggling for balance. This was also the "program" I had been on for the five days prior to meeting Nina for my interview. I was bloated, tired, and hadn't been eating well. The irony of ironies, I was there to talk about my success with my fitness and health routine!

Well my moment arrived. I walked into the gym and there stood Nina Rowan Heller. I had only seen Nina in pictures and she was even more beautiful in person. She was 5'10"; had long, lean muscles, blonde hair, tan skin, and a warm smile. I was greetedwith a hug and invited to take a seat. We started to chat about my life and my experience with real estate. She asked numerous questions and seemed genuinely interested. We continued to talk, and while I was happy to get to know her, truth be told, I kept wondering when we would start shooting the video.

I remember trying to suck in my stomach as I talked to her. I was embarrassed about the weight I had gained and wondered if she would notice. As we continued to talk, I realized we were talking less about my career and more about my personal life. I later found out that Nina had a background in social work.

While I was really appreciative of her wanting to know more about me, I began to fixate on why we weren't starting to record anything. After all, that was why I was there! And then it happened… Nina grabbed my hand, held it in both of hers, and ever so gently broke the news that we would not be shooting that day.

A Pivotal Conversation

Nina proceeded to have a very open and honest conversation with me. I didn't realize it at the time but this conversation would turn out to be one of two events that would shift my life enormously. She first wanted to know what the last three years had been like for me. She then wanted to know how my heart was doing. She also asked how much sleep I was getting and how much water I was drinking per day.

As our conversation progressed, I opened up and told her about my divorce and how I was battling feelings of guilt and self-doubt. I was working way too many hours and not sleeping enough. I was suffering from headaches and washing down one Advil after another with coffee. I was putting convenience and time concerns ahead of smart food decisions and I was just plain tired. I had a growing business but my life was way out of balance. I wasn't putting my health or well-being first any longer.

When I walked out of that room, I remember feeling deflated, embarrassed, sad, slightly confused, and very touched by Nina's care and concern. What it boiled down to was that a video of this point in my life would not match up with my words and actions. I was out of alignment with the very principles I was to be teaching. I talked a lot about taking care of myself and the importance of it but my reality was a different story. I was talking the talk, not walking the walk. That day with Nina was a big lesson for me.

Driven

To fully grasp why this was such a huge deal, you should know a little background on me. I am a driven woman. I always have been. I have never held a job where I didn't receive a promotion by the end of my third month. I give my all to my career. I also love people and genuinely feel happier when I make others happy. When I'm able to help others achieve their dreams, I'm my happiest!

When I found my career in real estate, I realized I could put my two greatest passions together. I could build relationships with people and help them find their dream home! I decided to get into real estate full time soon after this and partnered with my best friend Matt. Together we created The Aitchison & Adams Real Estate Team. Matt and I had big goals, so that meant big sacrifices were going to be made to achieve them. We worked extremely hard for those first few years… harder than I have ever worked in my life. I finally found something that made me feel fulfilled.

The problem was, it was not a well-rounded fulfillment! I married young and married someone I had little in common with. Consequently, I experienced many challenges during this period. I knew that marriage wasn't necessarily easy but I was completely unprepared for what I had. After quite a bit of counseling, and years of trying, my marriage ended and I was deeply heart broken.

When I got divorced, I realized I was tired of the kind of life I had been living. Not knowing another way, I simply pushed my feelings down in order to focus on the one thing I could control, my business. With this formula, my business kept growing. I was so engrossed in my career, and seeming happiness, that I started to think I WAS my career.

A Hungry Black Hole

In a nutshell, I was putting all of my happiness and energy into growing my business. As a result of its continued growth, I thought all was well. What I finally realized during my talk with Nina was that when you don't deal with your issues, they don't go away. They will simply lay dormant until you wake up pounds heavier and notice all may not be as it seems! Feelings ignored tend to build and fester. With me, that festering turned into a hungry black hole that was determined to take me down. When you don't deal with your issues, they don't go away.

When you don't deal with your issues, they don't go away.

People tend to numb out when they are in pain in order to function. They start doing things to distract themselves from having to deal with what is really going on. This is done in all sorts of ways: excessive drinking, eating, drugs, shopping, working, video games, television, Internet, etc.

When I took a look at my life, I realized I distracted myself in two major ways: dating and drinking. In my industry, "Happy Hour" was a regular part of winding down a busy day. I was also back into the dating scene and really longing to be in a relationship. What this translated into was one to two dates a week, plus a girls' night out on the weekends. I was drinking a minimum of three nights a week. It didn't seem like that big of a deal initially. However, when I actually looked at it, it was adding up to a bottle and a half of wine per week, plus an additional cocktail or two. Did you know that works out to 1,184 calories? I sure didn't! And let's be honest, after a couple of glasses of wine, those french fries look pretty darn good, and so does dessert!

Lost to Found in 90 Days: Chapter 1

Welcome to 30

Now this brings me to the second event in my life that created a monumental shift. I flew from Texas, where I left Nina, directly to San Diego to celebrate my thirtieth birthday with my best friend Katie. Thirty! I had always thought thirty sounded so old. And here I found myself turning thirty. As a kid, I remember thinking there were certain milestones you hit as an adult. Once you hit those, you would presumably be happy. To me they entailed finding a career you loved, getting married, buying a dream home, and having kids. I never planned on my marriage ending. Who does?

So I found myself in San Diego, turning thirty, and needing to get ready for my big night out. I put on a really cute, white, lace dress I had bought for the occasion. I remember thinking, "Oh my God! This is NOT how I remember this dress looking! Whose stomach is this? Yikes!! I look like a puffer fish! I hope the club's lighting is dark."

We ended up having a great time and stayed out until the wee hours of the morning. As we were flying home, I started to think about those milestones. I did have the career I loved but no longer had my marriage or my dream house. And kids… well that was going to be a while. Everyone had told me that my thirties were going to be the best years of my life. Well, I didn't feel like I was off to a great start.

And then it happened. Katie and I were sitting next to each other on the plane and I asked to see the photos from the night before. As we were flipping through, I saw a picture that made my jaw literally drop. Who was that girl? I didn't even recognize myself anymore. I had extensions in my hair (worst idea ever), was bloated beyond belief, AND let's just say the lighting did not cooperate with my master plan! Honestly, I looked awful. I was overweight, wearing a fake smile, and more than anything, I really, really looked like I needed a nap!

I can't quite explain it, but sitting on that plane, I made a substantial pact with Southwest Airlines and myself. I was done being the girl who always complained about her weight and feelings. I would do something about them!

I had a life to lead. I wanted to feel good. I wanted to look good. I have always had big goals for myself professionally, but it was time for me to make some big PERSONAL goals and stick to them! I wanted to fall in love, but not the kind of love you might be thinking. I wanted to fall in love with myself! This was supposed to be a happy time in my life. I was going to go find my happiness.

When I embarked on this journey with myself, I had no idea the impact it would have on my life or that it would turn into this program. All I knew was that I wasn't happy with where I was and I wanted to change. I knew it wouldn't be easy, but nothing ever worth it is. Right?

Will it be easy? Nope.
Will it be worth it? Absolutely!

Lost

I started to think about what was holding me back from being the highest and best version of myself. I knew that part of my life was on track because I was traveling all over the US coaching others on how to build a successful real estate business. However, the things that really mattered, the things that define what makes a person successful, were totally lost on me. I use the word "lost," because that is how I felt. I decided it was time to dig deep. And the deeper I dug, the more confused I became! I had a great career, an amazing group of friends, was relatively healthy, and even lived in a perfect neighborhood surrounded by happy families. Not bad at all! Yet in spite of these blessings, I wasn't happy on a fundamental core-level. Since I love to laugh and have a good time, and tend to look on the bright side of things, this was a major surprise for me to uncover.

When I realized that the root of my problem was that I lacked SELF-LOVE, I unlocked the key for acquiring happiness deep down within me. Self-love is, in fact, what generates that core-level of happiness I was searching for – the kind of happiness that generates peace of mind, an open heart, and mental clarity. I had always thought I was a nice person and a good friend to others but that's not what I was searching for. I wanted to be one of those women who loved herself and accepted herself with all of her flaws and truly experienced inner peace.

Found

I needed to do something drastic! For a big change to take place, something big needed to shift. I decided on doing something that seemed simple at the time. I would take out the two loudest "noises" in my life, my two biggest distractions. I was hoping that the quiet I would find would help me learn more about the kind of love I needed to generate towards me, myself, and I.

On December 1, 2014, I committed to 90 days without dating or drinking. I informed my girlfriends of my plan. Some were excited, while others became annoyed. I told my parents and my business partner. I decided to let everyone in my immediate circle know my new plan so that I could be held accountable. I realized it would be harder to let my loved ones down than it would be to let myself down. Out of sheer instinct, I made accountability partners out of those who cared about me. I knew they wanted me to succeed.

Next, I decided that I should make my environment match my goals. I started to create a program that I would follow for the next 90 days. My goal was that by the end of the three months, I would look better, feel better, and reach a level of happiness that was beyond skin deep. If I was lucky, I might lose a few pounds, gain some clarity on the next stage in my life, and be a little closer to loving my thirties the way everyone had always said I would.

Lost to Found

What I didn't expect was that in the next 90 days, I would heal myself from the inside-out, start journaling, give myself to God, create a sacred space in my home, forgive myself for my divorce, define my standards for a future relationship, learn a new way of eating and maintaining health, lose 32 pounds, and finally, finally, finally… learn SELF LOVE!

Your Turn

Here's the deal: This book and program has been created for YOU! I couldn't go through something so major and life changing and not want to share it with others. My guess is that if you are holding this book, it is either because it was given to you as a gift by someone who loves and cares about you or you might be in the same "stuck position" that I was in. In this 90 day program, you will go on a journey with yourself. You will be on a path of self-discovery and learn the steps you need to reach your ultimate happiness.

There are two options for your participation here:

1. Read the Book, join the L2F90 Facebook Community, and have access to several exercises that I used through my journey.

2. Read the Book, join the Lost to Found Community, plus:
   - Access to the Lost 2 Found App
     - Grocery shopping lists
     - Tips on how to dress for your body type
     - Water/food/workout logs
     - An online journal
     - And much more!

- Connect with other Lost to Founders in a Private Online Community.
- Receive a weekly exclusive Inspirational Guidance Video that expands each chapter and dives into what you will experience that week.
- Participate in a daily 90 Day Facebook Challenge Accountability Group.
- Get a sporty Lost to Found T-shirt.

We want you to know that whatever option you choose, we are so excited that you decided to take this journey. Nina and I are elated to get to know you over these next 90 days! You will gain knowledge and insight about yourself that will help you throughout your whole life. You will gain clarity on *who* you want to become. You'll also have the opportunity to make friends for life in your new online community with other Lost to Founders all over the world. To learn more, visit www.lost2found90.com.

> When you make a post about your journey on Facebook, Twitter, or Instagram, make sure that you use **#L2F90** so that we can track your success!

Nina's Knowledge

Your Story

Your official starting point is now!
Rachel and I are excited to join you on this journey. Participate fully and it will lead to a dramatic change in your life.

Start where you are, with no judgment. This is really important to truly move forward. Don't focus on the past or the future but rather where you are in this moment! Skip the judgment and the feelings that go along with it. Judgment has a way of creating and perpetuating a cycle of learned helplessness. This is the opposite of what you need to move forward. Carrying judgment places a huge burden on yourself and requires energy that pulls you away from your goals. We are going to help you go towards your goals.

Self-Empowerment

This program is about empowering yourself to change. The key to moving forward on this 90 day journey of self-exploration is to acknowledge NOW as your starting point. It sounds simple but we all have so much history with our feelings and judgments, that this can be more difficult than we realize.

Think of the past as a savings account holding all of your vital information. This information can be cashed in for wisdom if managed correctly. This involves looking at it objectively from a neutral standpoint. Exploring our past, without criticism, can provide details for how to move forward. We want you to be able to look at your future armed with lots of information. The process of analyzing this information is much like on-the-job training for the next phase in your life. This program will help you reach your goals, take positive action, anticipate struggles, and avoid major pitfalls, by being well informed.

Your History as Information

So let's start cracking the code for a brave new you! Have you ever purchased a gym membership, only to use it for a short period of time and then not return? You wind up paying dues for years, in case you decide to go back. Or you find yourself paying a reduced monthly fee so that you can put your membership on hold, in order to keep the option available to come back sometime in the future. If this situation sounds familiar, you are not alone!

Here's what you really need to know about this scenario... Each time you think about your gym membership or the topic comes up in conversation, it will undoubtedly make you feel badly. And this will cost you personal power around this area in your life and possibly others. When I talk to new clients and they mention that they have a gym membership but haven't used it in a year, I watch them go from feeling badly to judging themselves harshly. So for your L2F90 journey, you are going to change this pattern!

Here's your opportunity to look at your gym membership history – or anything akin to this in your life – and chose to handle this as information to explore, rather than information to use against yourself. The more you explore objectively, the more valuable information you'll discover to help you shift. And the best way to explore is to ask yourself as many questions as possible regarding your situation.

Potential Starting Questions
What made me want to have a membership?
Have I been successful in the past going to the gym?
What did I do to be successful?
What happened that interfered with my success?
What do I like about the gym?
What do I dislike about the gym?
Has something changed that contributed to me not going to the gym?
If so, is there something I can do to rectify this?
What do I want to accomplish when I go to the gym?
Are there other ways to accomplish my fitness goals?
How is my health right now?
How is my energy level?

Every answer you give will provide you with important information. Maybe going to the gym isn't truly an option for you right now? Maybe your schedule is such that other solutions like online classes and meet-up groups in the park are more available to you? There are many solutions, and to find the best ones for you, you have to understand yourself and your situation.

Your Journey

It is commonplace to hear about people's transformative journeys to better health. These stories are used to motivate us into buying products and joining programs.

So how is this 90 day journey different? Lost 2 Found (L2F90) is entirely your journey and it includes a large community of L2F90 people in similar situations. You'll tap into a community that shares a hunger to transform and is there to support your efforts for positive change. You'll be able to relate to one another and have each other's backs throughout your 90 day journey.

Your Awareness

We want you to reach your true potential. This requires soul searching. Taking the time to observe and validate your experiences will be more powerful than you can imagine. If you've been depressed and feel success is out of reach, acknowledge your feelings without judgment. This is the start. Know that you are changing your situation and give yourself credit for taking steps toward positive change. As long as you stay out of self-judgment, you will be able to gain more and more power.

Here's a tip to get started. Phrases that begin with: "I should, I wish, I can't, I couldn't, I regret, I never, I always," are key phrases to help you recognize when you are in self-judgment. Remember that these phrases are as powerful, if not more powerful, as thoughts inside your head. Begin to catch yourself using these and you will know you are on the right track for change. Awareness is the first step. Re-phrasing will come next.

We want you to be able to look at your history with a new perspective. Your personal information awaits your curiosity and we're excited to see where this takes you. We assure you, this won't take long and we're very much looking forward to meeting the powerful you!

Ask yourself the following:
- What do you THINK you need to be successful?
- What do you FEEL would make you accomplish your goals?
- What have you SAID to yourself or to others about your current state?
- What is it that you BELIEVE you really need?

Consider the following as you dive into challenges:
- What are the OBSTACLES and CHALLENGES that have continually gotten in your way?
- What things have you DONE that you've had some success with or felt you could do?
- What things did you TRY that you weren't able to accomplish?
- What would you like to TRY, but are too afraid?

Remember to explore your past without judgment. Any challenge you may have had, any obstacle that you felt you couldn't tackle, all have solutions waiting for you to seize.

Know that the more you learn about yourself, your feelings, your reactions and responses to stress, your triggers, your relationship with food, your self-image, the societal influences on your health and perception of yourself, your beliefs, and your past challenges, the more you can liberate yourself from your past.

Self-knowledge is power. You're about to get very familiar with your story. And this is why this program will be different from anyone else's... because it is about you!

Your Accountability Partner and Community

During this journey we want you to be able to have what you need to succeed. An accountability partner is someone that you enter into an agreement with in order to keep each other accountable to what you agree upon. An accountability partner helps you keep your commitment. They remind, support, and encourage you throughout your journey.

Each week you will be reminded to engage with your accountability partner. If you are not in the online program, find a person in your life that is able to support you by texting you reminders and encouraging you. If you choose a partner in the L2F90 community, you will have someone that is also on a similar journey as you. Remember, often a person that you don't have a comfortable/familiar relationship with makes for a potent accountability partner.

Find a New Direction: Discover Your "Big Why"

Complete the L2F90 assessment as you start your journey.

What You Want
What was my catalyst for getting this book and starting this program now?
What do I want to happen with my health?
What do I want to happen with my body?
What else do I want?

Understanding You

What do you THINK you need to be successful?

What do you FEEL would make you accomplish your goals?

What have you SAID to yourself or to others around you about why you haven't managed to succeed long-term?

What is it that you BELIEVE you really need?

What are the OBSTACLES AND CHALLENGES that have continually come up that have hindered your success?

What things have you already DONE that you have had some level of success with?

What things did you TRY that you weren't able to accomplish?

Is there anything you FEEL you could do differently in order to succeed?

Self-Discovery
The more you know about yourself, the more tools you have on your journey.

Self-Reflection

What do I see when I look at my answers?

Do I have any patterns?

Are my responses the way I think of myself?

My Feelings

How do I feel about what I am discovering about myself?

What feelings seem to come up over and over again?

How have these feelings affected my actions?

My Reactions and Responses to Stress

What have I done in the past when I have been under stress?

What are the things that give me stress?

How do I handle my stress?

My Relationship with Food

What is my relationship with food?

Do I reward myself with food?

Do I eat when I'm emotional or to fill a void?

Do I eat mindlessly by zoning out in front of the TV?

Do I multitask when I eat?

Do I know what my body can digest and what it cannot (ie: food allergies)?

Do I eat foods that I know will make me feel badly?
My Self-Image
How do I feel about the way I feel?
How do I feel about the way I look?
How would I describe myself?
Societal Influences On My Health
What do I believe is impacting my health choices?
Where do I get my health information?
How does what others do in my inner circle, impact my plans for being healthy?
Societal Influences On My Perception
Do I compare myself to others? Who?
Who am I using as a standard measurement for me?
My Beliefs About My Physical Capacity and Limitations
What do I tell myself when I am exercising?
Who else do I hear in my head and what do they say?
What is my past experience with exercise and moving?
Do I have an injury or physical issue that affects me? How so?
My Support System and Level of Self-Compassion
Who speaks kindly to me about what I am taking on?
How am I supported by others verbally and physically?
How do I encourage myself?

Weekly Commitment

Your Activity

Write and sign a commitment and share it with your accountability partner/L2F90 Community. Address the following steps to build your foundation.

1. Your Official Starting Point
   - Create a powerful sentence that addresses your past as "information to help you move forward."

2. Your Journey
   - Describe the path that you see yourself on for this journey.

3. Your Awareness
   - What do you notice when you review your answers to the previous questions?
   - Do you see any patterns?

- Is there anything that surprises you?
- How would you describe yourself in a paragraph?
- Do you feel compassion for that person you described?
- If not, what would need to happen for you to feel compassion for yourself?

4. Your Accountability Partner and Community
- What do you need to feel safe in order to embark upon this journey?
- How can you get what you need to feel safe?
- Do you let others help you in any areas of your life?
- Do you believe that there are others like you that are in a similar position facing familar challenges and situations?
- Do you believe sharing your journey with others who are taking this journey could help you as well as them?

5. Understand Yourself and What You Want
Your "Big Why" is defined as WHY you do what you do. In other words, what motivates you? If you asked Rachel her "Big Why" for creating this program, she would tell you that she did it to inspire others to find the highest and best version of themselves, and to lead their best lives possible.
- Review your answers to the above questions aloud. Write a paragraph to describe what you learned about yourself.
- Do you know what your "Big Why" is? If not, what do you think it might be?
- Is there anything for which you would give up your "Big Why"? Are you feeling that your "Big Why" is powerful?

Your Accountability:
Connect with your accountability partner to exchange lists.

Your Journal

Keep a journal to capture your feelings, thoughts, observations, and "Aha" moments.

Include a Body Status Exam (BSE) in your daily entries - scan your body, head to toe, and check in with how your body is feeling.

Include a Mental Status Exam (MSE) in your daily entries - scan your mind/ thoughts, and check in with what you are thinking and feeling.

Your Thoughts and Notes:

Lost to Found in 90 Days: Chapter 1

Chapter 2:
Your Two Distractions

Rachel's Journey

I knew that I needed to do something drastic in order to generate a big life change. In retrospect, it is amazing how one snapshot in time could become such a powerful, motivating tool. I simply had to recall the memory of that thirtieth birthday photo and the fuel I needed to transform was generated. Instead of using the way I looked and felt to sabotage myself, I used it to catapult me forward. My journey to empowerment had begun.

Having recently gone to Nordstrom for that dreaded bigger size, I reflected. I had been a size 4-6 most of my life. I now found that my petite frame was carrying a surprising 162 pounds, and I was actually wearing a size 10. I knew that my pants had been fitting tighter and I wasn't feeling good about myself but seeing that picture made me aware of just how far I had traveled. I didn't even recognize myself anymore!

Clean Janine

One night while scrolling through Facebook, I made contact with a woman in my industry who recently lost a bunch of weight. She told me that she had lost her weight by going to a wellness clinic in Loomis, CA. At that point, I had tried every diet under the sun: no carb, low carb, cabbage soup, South Beach, Atkins, Eat Right for Your Blood Type, raw, broth, vegetarian...you name it. I was ready for a change. So, I made an appointment, walked into the clinic and was greeted by a lovely woman.

Janine told me about her program. She introduced me to the concept of eating whole, "clean" foods. Then came the kicker. She told me alcohol was NOT allowed in her program. Logically this made sense but I had never had to commit to this in such a formal manner. I listened to her protocol and wondered if I could really follow it. A moment later I found myself revisiting my thirtieth birthday photo and asked, "How long do I need to do this until I see results?"

Her answer surprised me. There were no money back guarantees and assurances that I'd lose seven pounds a week for the next six weeks. Instead, she looked me squarely in the eyes and said, "This is not a diet, it's a lifestyle change, so there isn't really a set time limit." To this I replied, "Yeah, I get that but if you had to put a time limit on it – for when I might see some results – what would that look like?" My results-oriented persistence had given me great, career success. However, Janine reiterated that this wasn't something that you began and finished. She emphasized that this program was an ongoing way of changing the way you live your life.

> This is not a diet;
> it's a **lifestyle change**.

I could see that I was going to have to spell it out for her. "Yes, I fully understand that, but you see, I am driven by goals and deadlines. I need to know an amount of time before I see results." Janine sighed. I could see that I was testing her patience but was also aware that she knew I was serious. "Ok, if you give me three months, I can change your life." And that was it. I committed on the spot. I would give her three months to transform my life.

A Recipe for Success or Failure

Then came the big realization. I didn't really think I drank that often but those three times a week added up. Remember that 1,184 extra calories a week? That's not a small number when you want to slim down. In light of the fact that it takes 3,500 calories to gain or burn off a pound, I now held the biggest clue to my weight gain. If I continued my old lifestyle, it would be a recipe for disaster.

I thought about all of those days that whirled by with my best intentions. I would wake up and that would be the day that I would start eating super healthy. I would eat clean! At 10:00 a.m. I'd be doing great until I discovered that someone had brought brownies to the office. I'd exercise control and only have one. I'd reassure myself that I could be healthy for the rest of the day.

This pattern would continue through lunch. If I ate Mexican food, I'd only have a few chips. By the time happy hour rolled around, I had already blown the day, so I'd have that one glass of wine and share an appetizer with friends. Of course, one glass of wine led to another. Does this sound familiar? At 162 pounds, I found myself definitely in need of that lifestyle change Janine was referring to.

Intentional Lifestyle Design

At that point I realized that if I was really going to transform my life, my environment was going to have to support my goals. I found out quickly that it was challenging to avoid alcohol at work functions, and awkward to avoid it on the dating scene.

Dating was an interesting experience for me. It had been a while since I had dated and I forgot how much energy it took. After a long day, the idea of heading out to a bar with friends in the hope of meeting someone special did not exactly appeal to me. In lieu of this, I decided to give online dating a try.

On a typical day, I worked hard, grabbed dinner after work, came home around 9:00 p.m., and logged onto a few dating sites. I found myself scrolling through men's profiles, judging whether or not a man might be a good fit for me. I'd listen to myself thinking, "Nope, I don't like his shirt" or "He's cute, I wonder if he is good father material?" Basically I was spending hours of precious time in this pursuit. There was no real connection or depth to this process at all.

Eventually, I had to concede that this mindless scrolling didn't feel good. This acknowledgement led me to my next epiphany. I was sitting in church one day when the Pastor began talking about how technology was running the lives of my generation. He said that if we really trusted God, we would put our faith in the idea that He had a path and a beautiful story planned for us. He challenged us to get off dating sites entirely and TRUST in GOD'S PLAN. He then talked about a book called When God Writes Your Love Story. Here's a section that seemed to speak directly to me.

*You continue to get your heart broken because you are holding the pen of your
life and trying to write your own story.
I am the Author of true love.
I am the Creator of romance. I know your heart's every desire.
I want to script a beautiful tale just for you, but first you must give the pen to Me.
You must let Me become the center of your existence. You must let Me have total control
of your love life, and every other area of your life as well.*

– From When God Writes Your Love Story by Eric and Leslie Ludy

Something clicked for me. I now knew what I had to do. For the next 90 days I would remove the two biggest distractions in my life: drinking and dating. On the spot, I pulled out my cell phone and deleted all of my dating apps. This felt surprisingly liberating.

Eliminating my two biggest distractions was one of the healthiest choices I ever made. It gave me a huge kick-start into a much better way of living.

Appetite for Distraction

Now let's bring things back to *you*. What are your biggest distractions? What are two things in your life that are holding you back from reaching your potential?
Let's go through an exercise to help you figure out what these two things might be.
Once you figure out these distractions, your world is set to change!

How to Identify Your Two Biggest Distractions

Visualize what a perfect life would look like for you. Picture having everything you've ever wanted and doing everything you've ever dreamed. How would that look and feel for you?

Now, in order for you to identify your two biggest distractions, you must determine what isn't working in your life. Write down your bad habits that prevent you from being more productive, fulfilled, and happier in general.

Next, make a list of ten things you might do differently or need to stop doing all together in order to improve your life. Here are some common examples:

Top Distractions
Lose 20 Pounds
Smoking
Not Attending Church
Drinking
Double Booking or Overcommitting
Video Games
Dating
Facebook
Soda
Pornography
Drugs

Examine your list of ten and pick your top two distractions. Which ones affect you the most by blocking you from reaching your goals and creating the life you really want? My guess is that as you were making your list, you knew which two stood out for you. Now we'll show you how to break it down even further and create an accountability plan.

Let's use two examples from above:

- Lose Twenty Pounds
- Video Games

In order to be successful removing a distraction, you need to get clear on how your distraction is preventing you from reaching your goal(s). Once you get clear, you can then set out to create a new environment that ensures your success. So you'll need to ask yourself some tough questions surrounding your distractions in order to create a plan of attack.

Lose 20 Pounds

If I choose to lose 20 pounds, I need to look at how I normally eat. What is my activity level? How much water do I consume a day? How many liquid calories do I consume? How many solid calories do I consume? How much sleep am I getting?

What snacks are in my cabinets and fridge? Do I socialize around food? What are my family and friends eating regularly?

Asking these kinds of questions will lead you to a clear picture of what you need to change. From this picture, you can form your plan. It's important to note, that in order to be successful, you don't want to go to extremes. Begin by making simple, effective changes. Start switching over to healthier food choices in general. Don't deny yourself everything you love, just start by substituting many of your unhealthy foods for healthy ones. As you start to make progress, you'll be surprised how much less you want those unhealthy choices.

The very first step in taking control of your environment is making sure your surroundings match up with your goals. Here are some possible steps you might take:

1. Remove white flour, white sugar, and fried foods from your diet and kitchen.
2. Start fresh! Toss out all processed snacks in cabinets and fridge.
3. Eliminate all calorie-laden beverages (soda, juice, etc.).
4. Limit your alcohol intake to two drinks per week.
5. Increase your water consumption to at least two liters per day.
6. Get a friend to join a gym with you and set up a regular workout routine.
7. Weigh and measure yourself once a week to track your progress.
8. Take "before and after" photos to see your progress.
9. Hang a photo on the fridge of your goal body image. Make sure the model is the same height and body type as you, so your goal is achievable. I know I won't be looking like Gisele anytime soon. She's 5'11" and this "tiny tot" comes in at a mere 5 feet!

Video Games

If I choose to stop playing video games, I need to look at how many hours of the day I'm playing these games in lieu of doing activities that will help me achieve my goals.

Questions to consider:

- How many hours do I play video games per day?
- How has playing video games negatively affected my life?
- Am I late to work because I stay up too late playing them?
- Do I always feel tired because I stay up late playing them?
- Am I meeting my responsibilities?
- Is my spouse or are my friends feeling upset because I'm not present?
- Do my kids not get the time they deserve with me because I "need" to reach the next level?

- Are my kids playing too many video games?
- What am I missing when I'm playing these games? Do I have an addiction to playing video games?

Some possible steps you could take:

1. Tackle your environment. Get the video game center OUT of your house. Don't just put it in the garage. Give it away or donate it. If it's within reach, even unplugged, you are leaving yourself open to temptation.
2. Make a list of things that bring you joy: hiking, biking, dining out, etc.
3. Make a list of things you want to bring into your life: Guitar lessons, painting lessons, church, joining a sports league.
4. Tell your friends what you are doing so that they can support you by not inviting you to game night!
5. Once you take away the things that distract you and start to replace them with more productive activities, you will find that your mindset follows these changes. You'll have more time to spend on things that actually give you a return. You'll find a deeper connection with yourself, a growing confidence level, and a new sense of freedom and self-worth.
6. Hint: If you ever find yourself saying, "I probably shouldn't..." or "I wish I didn't..." it's a good indication of a distraction holding you back from being the best version of you that you can be.
7. Once you identify your major distractions, remove them for the next 90 days. You will be amazed at the changes that take place!

Identify Your Two Biggest Distractions

Distraction 1
Distraction:
Why is this an issue for you? List it out.
How can your environment better support your goal?

Distraction 1

Create some steps for success around how to replace your distraction with more productive activities.

Find an accountability partner to help hold you accountable for the next 90 days (another L2F90 member or a friend).

Distraction 2

Distraction:

Why is this an issue for you? List it out.

How can your environment better support your goal?

Create some steps for success around how to replace your distraction with more productive activities.

Find an accountability partner to help hold you accountable for the next 90 days (another L2F90 member or a friend).

Nina's Knowledge: Your Two Distractions

What You Think

You've started to dig deeper and understand why you are where you are. In order to get to where you want to go, the next part of the equation is finding out what interferes with your goals. There are usually patterns of interruptions that keep you from achieving what you want. If you become aware of these patterns, you can begin to really identify your biggest distractions.

Frequently when I do client assessments, my clients will share their noble intentions. Great intentions without follow through create lots of emotions, mostly negative. These emotions often derail them from figuring out what it is that is preventing them from pursuing their goals.

For now, take a step back and view your life from an objective place, rather than an emotional place. Remember, don't judge yourself – you're simply gathering the information you need in order to reach your goals. This information will help you identify the distractions that interrupt your success.

Consider:
- Are you familiar with a pattern that interrupts your plans?
- Describe that pattern.
- What would the people closest to you say are your distractions?
- What is holding you back from success?

Find a New Direction: Examine What You Do

Now let's take an inventory on what you are doing, what you need to stop doing, and what you need to remove from your life altogether.

1. Fill in the chart below.

Your Do/Stop/Remove Chart		
Item:	Do, Stop, or Remove? (D/S/R)	Feelings associated with this:

2. After you fill in the chart, consider the following:

Overview
- How long have you wanted to stop or remove the above distractions from your life?
- Are there things that you would like to do less frequently?
- What are those things?

Stressors
- What do you consider to be the stressors in your life?
- Which stressors do you have control over?
- Which stressors does someone else have control over?
- Who has control over those stressors?

Obstacles
- What isn't working in your life?
- Which things that aren't working in your life do you have control over?
- Which things that aren't working in your life does someone else control?
- Who has control over the things that aren't working in your life?

Distractions
- What keeps you from doing what you want to do?
- Describe how this happens.
- Who keeps you from doing what you want to do?
- How do they do this?
- What do you want to change now?
- What do you want to change in the future?

What You Learned About Yourself
Fill in the blanks below
I am surprised to see
I didn't know that
I didnt realize how
I now understand
I can't believe
When I see my answers, I feel

3. Next, consider what you want.

List the things you would like to do, have, or create in your life. Use the table below.
- Rate each on a scale of 1-10 as to how important they are to you (1 being the least important and 10 being the most important).
- List your challenges in making this happen.
- List the things you need to make each happen.

Your Do/Have/Create Chart				
Item:	Rate 1-10	Want to Do, Have, Create	What You NEED To Make This Happen	Challenges

Now determine what your environment needs to be like for you to do the things you want, and have the things you desire. Truly understanding yourself and your life is the only way to make effective, long-term change.

Weekly Commitment

Your Activity

Knowing your health history as well as information about your current health status is important before launching into a fitness program of any kind. Use this opportunity to address any health questions, concerns, or issues. Now is the time to make sure you are up to date on your annual exams, blood work, etc. Accurate information is powerful. It will support your specific needs in order to ensure your success.

> ### Your Accountability:
> Review and discuss with your accountability partner and L2F90 Community how this week's exercises have made you feel and what you've discovered about yourself. Has anything really surprised you?

Your Journal

A Mental Status Exam or MSE is a tool that will help you gain a deeper level of self-awareness. Check in with your thoughts and record them so that you have a record of how your mind helps or hinders your ability to reach your goals.

By continually monitoring your daily MSE during your Lost to Found journey, you will be able to hear your inner dialogue and see how this affects your feelings and your ability to succeed. You'll know where your attitude comes from and you'll discover what you need to release in order to get out of your own way. This will help you move forward.

Document in your journal your MSE and what you are discovering about yourself. Include what you are doing now that is different from before, and what you have learned in the process.

Review all of your answers to this week's questions and start eliminating your two biggest distractions. Take this week to commit to your choices.

Write and sign a commitment and share it with your accountability partner and L2F90 Community.

Write your thoughts about your distractions. How did you choose your top two choices? How do you feel about removing them for 90 days?

- BSE – Body Status Exam – Check in with how your body is feeling.
- MSE – Mental Status Exam – Check in with what you are thinking.

Your Thoughts and Notes:

lost to found in 90 Days: Chapter 2

Chapter 3:
Your Day: Planning & Implementing

Rachel's Journey

Supporting Your Health in Your Daily Schedule

If you examine the people who have succeeded in this country at a high level, you'll notice they share a common practice. A few that really have influenced me: Bill Gates, Oprah Winfrey, Warren Buffet, and Gary Keller. These high-level achievers all get up early and have a set morning routine. I realized pretty early on that if I was going to commit myself to this 90 day challenge – while keeping up with my work schedule – I was going to need my own successful morning routine.

At about the same time, I encountered a book by Hal Elrod called, "The Miracle Morning." The book was filled with tips on how to create a powerful morning routine. Incorporating some of his ideas and some of mine, I had a powerful method for approaching my day.

I am actually not a natural early morning riser. My steady appearance at the office at 10:00 a.m. was a well-established routine. I realized that in order to be the best version of myself in this 90 day challenge, I needed to be the kind of person who got up earlier. That version of myself would need to rise a couple of hours earlier in order to include some empowering practices into my day. So I ventured into new territory with the goal of taking charge of my day at a higher level.

My Morning Routine

6:30 a.m.
Wake: Set alarm across room. Replace the snooze option with a forced march to turn it off. (Whatever it takes!)
Drink a full glass of water and brush my teeth. Your body can get dehydrated while you sleep. So before my two feet hit the floor, I chugged a glass of H20. I also realized the power of peppermint. Brushing my teeth first thing would not only wake up my taste buds but seemed to make me more alert and ready to focus. This made me less likely to get back in bed.

6:40 a.m.
Pray and Meditate: Included positive affirmations about who I was and how my day was going to be. This was a super important aspect of my practice. The only thoughts I allowed in my head were those involving the person I wanted to become.

7:00 a.m.
Journal: Write anything on my mind, including my goals, dreams, and what I was grateful for. This journal became my nonjudgmental best friend – another super important tool.

7:20 a.m.
Exercise: 25 squats, 22 push ups, 45 sit-ups – non-negotiable!

7:40 a.m.
Breakfast and Supplements: Fuel my body with the proper brain food.

8:00 a.m.
Shower: Dress and prepare for the day.

9:00 a.m.
Work: Arrive early to increase productivity.
In truth, my morning routine started with a few bumps. Sometimes I would skip my journaling, sometimes I would only do 10 push-ups, and once or twice I hit the snooze button and ran back to bed! The thing is, once I started seeing progress, my commitment rose steadily, as did my conviction. I realized I was only cheating myself when I didn't complete part of my morning ritual. With this attitude in mind, my morning routine got stronger and by the end of my 90 days, I remember thinking, "How did I ever sleep in before? I missed the most important part of the day!"

Starting your day with "intention" is so incredibly important. Creating a path to follow that supports the highest and best version of yourself and ensures your success in multiple areas of life. Rather than entering your day in a reactive state, your morning routine can have you enter it grounded, centered, and highly responsive. This will allow you the greatest ability to carve your own destiny and receive maximum benefits.

Remember this whole process is about you creating a "life by design." If you start your day off right, the rest of your day is much more likely to follow the same trend.

The Turbo Charged Calendar

Including Your Goals in Your Weekly Schedule

The next step for me was creating a weekly calendar that would help support my goals. Have you ever heard people say, "I want to do that, I just don't have enough time." Well, I fell into that camp. I always felt rushed. I felt like my time was too limited during the day and I often double booked myself. I fooled myself into thinking that if I just had more hours in the day, I would be so much more productive.

So let's look at the concept of double booking. Obviously, we can't be in two places at one time even if we want to be. There was a time when I was double booking myself a lot. A friend would ask me to attend a birthday party or networking event, and I wouldn't want to disappoint them (total people pleaser here) so I would say yes. I was double booking because I wasn't checking my schedule before committing.

The Challenge of Being a People Pleaser

When I double booked, I was aware that I might have to cancel but didn't want to let anyone down in the moment. The problem was, I was delaying the inevitable. I was going to have to cancel on someone. If I had looked at my calendar, I would have known if I had the time available to attend that party. I learned it is far better to give a "clean no" than a "dirty yes." When I gained clarity on this, I realized I wanted to be the kind of person people knew they could count on. I stopped making last minute cancellations and opted for total integrity. Doesn't your word matter?

I also remember thinking that my life was so "busy," and yet, at the end of the day I really hadn't accomplished that much! So what was it that I was so busy doing? We all have the same 24 hours in a day. Some just use theirs more effectively. I knew I wanted to accomplish a lot, so I committed to making the most of my 24 hours! This is when I was introduced to the wonderful world of time blocking.

Get a Clone or Get a Calendar

I decided to go to an office supply store and get a new calendar. I wanted to start fresh. I picked up some colored markers as well. Green was for money-making activities directly related to my real estate business. Purple was for personal activities. Yellow was for appointments I needed to attend that day. I started filling out my calendar with my non-negotiables. These included my powerful morning routine, uninterrupted client-prospecting time, my lunch break (a brain requires fuel!), etc.

I found that blocking activities in 1.5-hour time blocks was extremely effective, and ultimately played a key factor in improving my productivity. Consistency was another key factor. Every day started with my morning routine, followed by my real estate appointments that required an hour, plus a half hour for drive time. When I got clear on how many appointments I could keep each day, I got excited to fill them up! I even put in my calendar what time I would go home, have dinner, and spend time with my friends.

I noticed a huge shift when I followed my schedule diligently. Not only was I getting more accomplished during the day, but I had time left over! I was creating a life that was really starting to flow. With my extra time, I could continue to work or go read a good book in a coffee shop. I now had more options.

> **Time Blocking** - Not only was I getting more accomplished during the day, but I had time left over!

Me-Time

In addition to my health and work goals, I added one more component to my calendar, some "me-time." When I was married, my husband and I had a regular "date night." I kept this concept going; however, I allotted this time for taking care of myself. I would make sure to do something that was both enjoyable and relaxing. This is when I'd read a good book, catch a movie with a friend, or stay in for a candlelit bubble bath. I also made sure to allow one night a week to hang out with friends, only I replaced the wine with soda water and lemon!

Achieving balance in life is fundamental for health and well being. I realized that personal time was just as important as client appointments, in terms of creating a balanced and happy life. So remember to keep those appointments with yourself because you matter and you are worth time blocking for!

Rachel's Perfect Schedule	
Timeslot	Focus
6:30-8:30 a.m.	Power Morning – Workout & Water!
8:30-10:00 a.m.	Affirmations & Emails
10:00-11:00 a.m.	Lead Generation
11:00-12:00 a.m.	Lead Generation
12:00-1:30 p.m.	Lunch Appointment
1:30-3:00 p.m.	Appointment Slot
3:00-4:30 p.m.	Appointment Slot
4:30-6:00 p.m.	Appointment Slot
6:00-7:30 p.m.	Cook Healthy Dinner
7:30-10:00 p.m.	Family Time
10:00-11:00 p.m.	No Technology
11:00 p.m.	Bedtime

Write It Down

Now, what I'm about to introduce you to is simple, yet profound. For two days, I want you to record everything that you do from the time you wake up to the time you go to bed. EVERYTHING! If you hit the snooze button four times, write it down. If you schedule 20 minutes for breakfast but take 40 minutes because you are watching the latest YouTube video, write it down. If you get stuck in 30 minutes of traffic, write it down. If you have to run across town to drop a package off at FedEx, write it down. You are truly writing down everything you do for two days. Once you've done this, I want you to take a careful look at your last two days and analyze them. Determine what you are doing each day and how you are spending your time.

I put myself through this exercise when I was feeling so hurried and busy and not accomplishing a lot. I had to take a HARD LOOK at how I was spending my time. During those two days of recording my daily activities a particular incident provided me with important information. I received a call from a client. They had changed their plans and wanted their house put on the market a day earlier. This required that I place a lockbox on their property immediately. I was pretty slammed that day but it needed to get done. Their house was across town and it took me a half hour to get there. Coming back, I hit traffic. By the time I returned to my office, I had used an hour and a half of time that I hadn't planned on. I remember how frustrated I was when I added this to my daily log. It felt like I had lost a valuable chunk of time in the middle of my busy day.

*I had to take a hard look
at how I was spending my time.*

The Value of Your Time

This is when the magic happened. I decided to look at how that 1.5 hours out of my day really affected my overall output. To do this, I determined my hourly rate. I divided the income I earned that year by 2,000 (removing two weeks for vacation, I multiplied 50 weeks per year by 40 hours of work per week = 2,000 hours of work per year). I was stunned to find out the value of my time! Had I not done this exercise, I would never have realized that lockbox cost me $190.00. I finally knew what my time was worth!

I then created a "START/STOP/CONTINUE List."

In my START column, I put all the things I wasn't doing that I needed to start. These were the activities that would increase my productivity. For you, it might be time blocking or saying morning affirmations.

In my STOP column, I put all the things I needed to stop doing during my working hours or delegate to someone else (i.e., hire a runner for the lockbox delivery!). In my CONTINUE column, I put all the activities I was doing well that were promoting my success. This column is a great bolster. Often we are too hard on ourselves. This is the column that verifies that we are doing good work when we may not necessarily give ourselves the credit.

When my list was complete, I circled all the things I was doing that were not actively making me money. I realized It would have been more cost effective to pay a runner $25 to go drop off the lockbox. Had I not done this exercise, I would have found that expense "unnecessary," when in fact, it was the best choice.

Carefully examining how I was spending my working hours had a powerful affect on my business. The new level of clarity I gained on what I needed to do (and not do) in order to be successful, now made me hyper-productive and ultimately helped me achieve my goals. What a domino effect! I made sure my working hours were spent performing "dollar producing activities."

Start	Stop	Continue

Download Your Start/Stop/Continue List

To download your Start/Stop/Continue List visit:

http://www.lost2found90.com/start-stop-continue

Pursue Your Ideal

I realized quickly that if I squandered time, I would never meet my goals. However, if I packed it with productive activities, I would consistently have positive results. In light of this, I wanted to make the most of my time. So after knowing how I needed to fill my day, I created my ideal, weekly calendar chock full of activities that would support my sales objectives and my health.

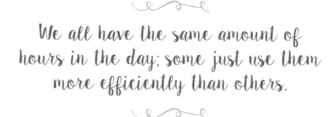

We all have the same amount of hours in the day; some just use them more efficiently than others.

Once you are armed with the information you gain from your SSC List, there's one more step I'd like you to add to your valuable day. This is a very effective and easy way to begin and end your day and has the potential to really shape your 90 day challenge. When I consistently used this exercise as a daily measuring tool for my productivity, the results I had were amazing.

Look at your day through goal-driven, solution-based lenses and try this repeatable 4-step process. It worked wonders for me and can do the same for you!

Your Four Steps to Success

Make sure to include this in your journal.

Nina's Knowledge: Planning and Implementing Your Day

Create Your Powerful Calendar

When I started my health consulting business, it was really important to me to meet the needs of people that weren't ever getting to the gym. I had been lifting weights and working out in gyms for years and knew that a very small percentage of people with memberships consistently went to the gym. I was determined to eliminate this obstacle for my clients and decided to provide in-home personal training and coaching services.

It gave me so much satisfaction to help people that I struggled with turning away clients. Finally, I had to create a wait list because I realized I could not add one more client to my day. I was already working more than 14 hours a day. When my business reached this point, it forced me to get very focused and organized with my calendar. During those early years I would often have 12 to 14 clients a day. In order to drive to client's homes, have an hour appointment and then drive to the next client's home, I used a couple of tools.

Power(ful) Tools

1. **Alarm watch**

   I would set my alarm at the beginning of each session as I checked in with clients. This was a very effective way to make me aware of when it was time to wind down the appointment. I set my watch to beep 9 minutes before the session ended to give me time to close our training session. This not only helped me to wrap things up in a timely manner but let my clients know their workout was almost done.

   There are so many great technological options to use now in order to keep you on task and on time. Make the best use of your smartphones, apps, watches, etc. to support your time boundaries.

2. **Appointment book**

   I recorded every client appointment and all of my errands. To train as many clients as I could and make the most of my time, I wrote everything in my calendar. I based my schedule on client locations in order to minimize travel time. I got so organized that for years, I actually managed to have 8 clients living next door or across the street from one other. This reduced my travel time down to five minutes each. Twenty years later, I use my phone and computer to schedule everything. However, it's not a bad idea to have a paper backup. Technology has a way of crashing sometimes and having a hard backup calendar can save your day and week!

It was easy to track client sessions for billing purposes because everything was accounted for in my calendar. I also used my calendar to record tasks that I needed to do for each client for the following week.

My clients have been some of the most successful professionals in Austin and I deeply respect their time and feel compelled to keep good boundaries with each appointment. I could not have done this without these tools.

My business needs challenged me to use my time extremely efficiently. Understanding your specific needs will help you to create a system that works best for you. If you don't currently have a powerful calendar, look at how you spend your hours and see what you need to do to increase your performance. The more information you have, the more successful you will be at creating optimal solutions.

Understanding You and Your Day

Your Calendaring Worksheet

In order to prioritize your most important activities and manage your time effectively, you need to know how you are really spending your time. Seeing what you are doing on an hourly basis will enable you to make better choices. Once you do this, you can structure your day to match what you want to achieve.

Your Day					
5 a.m.		**1 p.m.**		**9 p.m.**	
5:15		1:15		9:15	
5:30		1:30		9:30	
5:45		1:45		9:45	
6 a.m.		**2 p.m.**		**10 p.m.**	
6:15		2:15		10:15	
6:30		2:30		10:30	

Your Day					
6:45		2:45		10:45	
7 a.m.		**3 p.m.**		**11 p.m.**	
7:15		3:15		11:15	
7:30		3:30		11:30	
7:45		3:45		11:45	
8 a.m.		**4 p.m.**		**12 a.m.**	
8:15		4:15		12:15	
8:30		4:30		12:30	
8:45		4:45		12:45	
9 a.m.		**5 p.m.**		**1 a.m.**	
9:15		5:15		1:15	
9:30		5:30		1:30	
9:45		5:45		1:45	
10 a.m.		**6 p.m.**		**2 a.m.**	
10:15		6:15		2:15	
10:30		6:30		2:30	
10:45		6:45		2:45	
11 a.m.		**7 p.m.**		**3 a.m.**	
11:15		7:15		3:15	
11:30		7:30		3:30	
11:45		7:45		3:45	
12 a.m.		**8 p.m.**		**4 a.m.**	
12:15		8:15		4:15	
12:30		8:30		4:30	
12:45		8:45		4:45	

After you have documented your day, look at your calendar and ask yourself the following questions:

- What do you notice about how you are spending your time?
- Do you see patterns?
- Are you doing what you need to do throughout the day?
- Do you have long "To Do" lists at the end of the day?
- What are the things that take your attention away from what you need to accomplish?
- Are you prioritizing your most important activities?
- Are the things you are doing related to your goals?

Find a New Direction: Manage Your Time

Your Alarms

Find an alarm system that keeps you on track throughout your day. There are many options out there. Make sure to choose one you can adhere to. If you work with people, this can help your clients know that it's time to wind things down.

Look at your Calendaring Worksheet to determine what supports you:

- How do you know when it's time to change activities?
- How do you make the transition from one appointment or activity to another?
- Who or what other tools support you to accomplish what you need to throughout your day?
- Do you pay for that person or those services?
- How much do they cost?
- What else do you need to help you utilize your time more efficiently?

Sacred Use of Time

Sacred activities are things that are highly valued and important to you. They feed your body, mind, and soul. In order to make your day powerful, make sure to include this category in your calendar. These activities are the ones that empower you. Often it is your simple pleasures that provide you with energy, stamina, joy, bliss, and passion. Consider these questions about your use of time.

- What are your sacred activities?
- Do these activities nurture and empower you?
- Do these activities give you energy, joy, and a sense of well being?
- List your passions_____

If you need help determining your passions, answer the passion questions below.

Passion Questions
What makes you smile?
What gives you energy?
What do you feel you have a passion for (writing, music, art, movies, travel, sports, friendships, work)?
Have you ever felt bliss?
What gives you your drive?
Is there something that gets you out of bed in the morning or gives you what you need to do the things that you don't want to do?
What moments in your day give you peace, pleasure, and enjoyment?
What are the simple things that give you joy?
If you were given 30 minutes in the middle of your work-day to do anything, how would you spend them?
What are the things you enjoy doing on vacation?
How great would you feel if you included one or more of the above in your weekly calendar?

Treat Your Calendar as an Indispensable Assistant

There is a misconception that including everything in your calendar will make you feel even more pressure. It actually has the opposite effect. Having a detailed schedule supports and protects you.

Think of your calendar as an indispensable assistant you don't have to pay! If you're a people pleaser and have a hard time saying no, your calendar can save you. If, for example, a person asks you to join a committee and you're already feeling overwhelmed and know you don't have time for one more commitment, your calendar can provide your guilt-free "no!"

Here's a typical scenario that plays out… You're pulling into your garage when a neighbor "ambushes" you.

"Hi! We'd love for you to participate on the neighborhood planning committee."

You'll notice this has not been phrased as a question. You've now been caught off guard and the fact that you care about the neighborhood makes it that much harder for you to advocate for your time.

Your neighbor has already assumed you are perfect for the committee and has practically included you without your response. And here's how your trusty calendar can save the day...

You calmly take out your calendar and ask, "When does the committee meet and how many hours a week are required? Once your neighbor hears this, they will already know how seriously you take your time commitments and how stretched you probably are.

Then you can answer by saying, "Let me look at my calendar. I'm sorry. I already have a standing appointment at that time and need to meet a work deadline that is taking up all of my free time. I know this is important and I appreciate that you're all taking such good care of the neighborhood. Thanks for thinking of me." Learning to provide simple answers with less personal information is also a powerful way of defending your time boundaries without someone trying to encroach upon them. The more personal information you arm others with, the more opportunity you give them to push your boundaries. It may take practice to respond succinctly but the payoff is significant. You'll accomplish what you need to, meet your goals, and avoid getting side tracked.

Results of an Effective Calendar

Your effective calendar does many positive things.

- It makes you a priority. Your health, food, exercise, and sacred activities will energize you and keep you in balance. This will support your growth.
- It supports you as you master the skill of using your calendar to stay on task. Use it for guidance and support daily.
- Your personal power and confidence builds from doing what you say you are going to do. Follow through with all of your commitments.
- An effective calendar gets rid of "blind spots and fantasies" in your schedule. These are the appointments/events that you put in your calendar that you have no intention of keeping. If you don't have the time to go to the gym, take it off your calendar rather than turning a blind eye to it and feeling badly at the end of the week. These types of entries take away your power. Again, follow through with everything in your calendar.

Change, great intentions, and healthy interventions don't have a chance when they don't have a place in your schedule. Creating a calendar that supports you and your growth makes you more powerful and determines your success.

Your Weekly Commitment

Your Activity

Create your powerful calendar – and follow it!

- Review your answers in this chapter to create your new calendar.
- Include your sacred appointments.
- Follow your calendar.
- Have a printed version of your daily calendar to jot down notes on how you're doing.
- Create your alarm system to keep you on task.

Your Accountability:
Share your calendar with your accountability partner.

Your Journal

Journal how you are feeling, thinking and any observations you've made regarding your new "Aha" moments.

- BSE – Body Status Exam – Check in with how your body is feeling.
- MSE – Mental Status Exam – Check in with what you are thinking.

Your Thoughts and Notes:

Lost to Found in 90 Days: Chapter 3

Chapter 4:
Your Water

Rachel's Journey

Water! Oh that dang H20! I have always known that water was important. I have heard it since I was a kid, "Drink your 8 glasses a day!" Truth be told, I have never been a person who enjoyed water. It is not that I don't like the taste of water. I just tend to get busy and am not aware of being thirsty. When I am aware of being thirsty, I tend to want alternatives to water.

Nina has many intuitive gifts and on the day that I met her in Texas, back in October of 2014, I was surprised by how much we wound up talking about water. During that first meeting, I discovered how perceptive she was at reading people's energy. She literally reads people for a living and knew that my body wasn't happy or running at an optimal level. Once she keyed into this, she had no intention of talking to me about business. What she did want to discuss was the root of why my body was struggling at the time.

When in Texas...

I remember thinking, "Water is just water." I had NO idea that it would end up being the foundational building block that would position me to start making one healthy-living choice after another. So when Nina asked me how much water I was drinking per day, I sheepishly looked away. I knew it wasn't nearly enough. In coming up with an answer, I suddenly became aware of how many cups of coffee and cocktails I had consumed over the past several days while attending the conference. I also realized that my food choices involved a lot of fried foods and amazing BBQ. Come on… when in TEXAS! So our conversation went something like this:

Rachel: "Um … I know I'm not drinking enough water. Maybe a few glasses?"

Nina: "And how much coffee would you say you drink per day?"

Rachel: "Oh, maybe two cups a day?"

Nina: "Give me your hand."

At this point she gently reached for my hand and held it in front of her. She proceeded to lightly pinch the skin on the back of my hand and said to me, "Rachel, do you see this? Your skin is supposed to go back down. Do you have any idea how dehydrated your body is?" I really didn't but in hindsight I was significantly dehydrated.

Nina continued to ask me how I was feeling physically and what my energy level was like. She also wanted to know if I was getting headaches or body aches and whether my appetite seemed normal. As I thought about the answers to these questions, I realized that I didn't feel very good. I was tired, bloated, had a headache, and really just wanted to crawl into a hole and hide.

Hydrolyzed Environments, Your Cells, and You

Nina explained to me that our bodies are made up of 60% water, and that our cells are only able to function properly in a hydrolyzed environment. This requires proper fluid intake. She stressed the importance of maintaining balance by drinking water throughout the day. Cells literally cannot perform their functions without enough water, and we tend to get toxic quickly when we are dehydrated. Kidneys require water to flush toxins out. I instantly envisioned a beach covered with flopping fishes and no ocean in sight. No wonder why I was feeling less than my best!

The final verdict was when Nina looked me straight in the eye and said, "Rachel, you are a driver. You are a motivated woman who is going places. If you do not hydrate your body and give your cells what they need, your body won't be able to support you." This stopped me dead in my tracks. I had BIG goals for myself. I had places to go, houses to sell, and a world to influence! Water was not going to slow me down!

I realized the profound importance of what Nina was saying, when I recalled that I had been hospitalized twice during my college years for dehydration. Yes, this is quite the extreme example but it wasn't until this moment in time that it really clicked. I was finally ready to hear this information in a way I hadn't had access to before. Obviously, I really needed to pay attention to my body's call for water.

It's amazing how you can hear the same information over and over again but it doesn't sink in until you are ready to receive it. I was finally ready. Even if being hospitalized didn't get it through my head, seven years later being told I wasn't going to hit my goals unless I changed my ways did it for me! Water… I finally got it!

My Water Promise

It was in that moment that I made a pact with Nina to drink two liters of water every day. I would follow through with this because I made a promise to both Nina and myself. She then asked me for a commitment out loud. So I made the commitment out loud and I kept it.

One thing I learned from Nina involving water and travel is that our bodies get dehydrated easily when we fly. To combat this, the very first thing she does when she gets through security in an airport is to grab the largest bottle of spring water she can find. Her rule is, by the time your plane hits the ground, you make sure you've finished that bottle. I now do this every time I fly. I call it, "Nina's Rule!"

> **Nina's Rule:** By the time your plane hits the ground, you make sure you've finished that bottle!

Your Temple

Nina talked to me about treating my body like a temple. "Treat your temple right," she would remind me. When I think of a temple, I think of a beautiful building with elegant peaks and stained glass windows sparkling in the sunlight. If you owned that temple and it was your job to make it shine, you would clean it daily and make sure it was well respected. So treat your body like YOUR temple. Respect it and let it reflect how well you care for it.

Nina's Knowledge: Water

For over 20 years working with clients and speaking to groups, there have been common questions that people often ask. One of the most frequent questions is, "What is the simplest thing I can do right now that will make a big impact on my health?" I have two answers to that question. The first one is to drink more water. The second is to walk every day. Let's talk about water for now.

Your Resistance to Drinking Water

Have you ever questioned yourself as to why you resist drinking water? It may sound absurd but many people have resistance to increasing their water intake. Surprisingly, it is one of the most frequent challenges people share with me. The three most common responses that I hear when people say they can't drink more water are:

- I don't have time to keep going to the bathroom.
- I don't have water handy.
- I don't like the taste of water.

Your Objections	
Do you have resistance to drinking more water?	
What is your reason you don't drink more water?	
What do you like to drink?	
What do you seem to drink the most?	

People often have resistance to drinking more water until they understand the importance of this. If you could take a pill that would aid your health, you would have to have a glass of water to take the pill. Think of getting hydrated as something easier than taking a pill. You can skip the pill altogether. Everyone is always looking for the easiest and fastest intervention that will result in a big impact on his or her health. Water is your ticket!

Observing Your Body

Check in with your body. Do you have any of these symptoms?

List of Symptoms	Daily	Weekly	Monthly	Yearly
Headache				
Muscle Aches/Pains				
Joint Pain				
General Pain				
Fatigue				
Dry Skin				
Constipation				
Dizziness				
Afternoon Lulls				
Dry Mouth				
Dark Urine				
Increased Thirst				

Everything listed in this chart is a symptom of being dehydrated.

- What do you notice about yourself?
- Do you see any patterns?
- Are you surprised?
- Do you have any recurrent symptoms?

Our healthcare system encourages us to treat our symptoms with medicine. However, this approach doesn't address the root cause of our symptoms. In fact, most often, medicine masks our symptoms and never addresses the imbalance that is creating the symptom in the first place. As a result, many people will choose a painkiller for a headache that is caused by dehydration. And many people will grab a cup of coffee to give themselves an energy boost, when their fatigue is due to dehydration. Drinking water throughout the day is actually what is needed to avoid these symptoms altogether and stop them from recurring. So don't make substitutions for water. It's a far healthier fix and it's fast and easy!

Understanding Hydration

I like to keep things simple. It is helpful to educate yourself in order to create healthy habits. There are some basics about your body's water requirements that can help you shift your mindset about drinking enough water.

- The human body is more than 60% water.
  - Blood is 92% water.
  - Brain and muscle tissue are 75% water.
  - Bones are approximately 22% water.
- A human can survive for a month or more without eating food but only a week without drinking water.

The body is amazingly complex. Hydration, or lack thereof, will support or hinder cellular function. Cells contain water and are surrounded by water. When dehydrated, cell membranes become less permeable. This slows vital hormones and nutrients from entering cells. This also prevents waste products that cause cell damage from flowing out of cells.

When your body isn't functioning optimally at the cellular level, you may not have symptoms that you can identify immediately but the imbalances are still present. Basically, your cells won't be able to do their jobs optimally. To understand the impact of what is happening in your body, consider the following. Heart rate and blood pressure increase with dehydration. The brain itself does not get enough blood when you are dehydrated, and this compromises every system it runs. This is why when you are dehydrated you will often feel faint and dizzy when you stand up. In addition, your digestion, energy level, brain function, muscle function, and other systems will all be impacted by this. So you can see just how significant being hydrated is.

Benefits of Hydration
Detoxification
Appetite Suppression
Digestive Support
Improved Metabolism
Improved Muscle Performance
Good Sleep
Energy

Find Your New Direction: What I Need to Be Motivated

Calculate your personal water needs.

Your Personal Water Needs	
What is your current weight in pounds?	
Divide your weight by 2	
This is how many ounces of water you need per day. (This is the low end of the scale)	

Working out, intense weather, medications, diuretic drinks, etc. all will impact the amount of water you need per day.

Sample plan:
Drink the majority of your water intake before 6:00 - 8:00 p.m. Keeping this timeframe can reduce bathroom visits in the middle of the night.

- 50 oz. by noon, 50 oz. by 6:00 p.m.
  OR
- 25 oz. by 10:00 a.m., 50 oz. by noon, 75 oz. by 2:00 p.m., 100 oz. by 6:00 p.m.

Some tips for your water intake

- I have filtered water at home. I drink out of a water bottle that I place 6 rubber bands on each morning. Each time I fill it, I remove a rubber band.
- When the rubber bands are gone, I've reached my goal.
- Replace carbonated beverages and fruit juices with water.
- Avoid diuretics (dehydrators) like caffeine and alcohol.
- When I travel, I use an app that helps me track my water intake.

Water is the foundation to great health. Getting hydrated is one of the easiest and quickest interventions to improve your health.

Weekly Commitment

Your Activity

- Look at Your Resistance to Drinking Water
  - ☐ List what motivates you to be sufficiently hydrated
  - ☐ Have the list available to see on a daily basis or as a reminder in your phone.

- Observe Your Body
  - ☐ Do you have frequent symptoms that give you concern?
  - ☐ Create a list of your symptoms. Rate each symptom's severity on a scale of 1-10. Monitor and rate those symptoms at the end of each day.

- Understand the Benefits of Hydration
  - ☐ What are the two most important benefits of being hydrated for you specifically?
  - ☐ On a scale of 1 to 10, how important do you believe being hydrated is for you?

- What I Need to Be Hydrated and My Water System
  - ☐ Water goal – Drink ½ your body weight in ounces.
  - ☐ Establish a hydration plan (schedule, bottles, preparation).
  - ☐ _____ Oz. by noon, _____ oz. by 6:00 p.m.
  - ☐ _____ Oz. by 10:00 a.m., _____ oz. by noon, _____oz. by 2:00 p.m., _____ oz. by 6:00 p.m.
  - ☐ For Home, Office, and Car: Be prepared, buy your water, have filtered water accessible, always have it with you, including travel bottles.
  - ☐ Share this with your people you spend time with – it will help support you and remind you to make this a habit.
  - ☐ Set up a system to track and remind you (you can use specific bottles, the rubber band system, apps, your accountability partner, etc.)

> ### Your Accountability:
> Connect with your accountability partner to support reaching your hydration goal for each day.

Your Journal

In your journal document how you are feeling and thinking. Make sure to include your observations and "Aha" moments about your water intake. Notice your current patterns and habits versus your old ones. Look for information to adjust your plan if needed.

- BSE – Body Status Exam – Check in with how your body is feeling.
- MSE – Mental Status Exam – Check in with what you are thinking.

Your Thoughts and Notes:

Lost to Found in 90 Days: Chapter 4

Chapter 5:
Your Nutrition and Fuel

Rachel's Journey

FOOD! Oh my goodness. This one's a biggie for me. To say that I have had a love affair with food is an understatement. I was raised in a home with an amazing mother who doubled as a gourmet chef for a family of 5. I learned at the age of three how to cook lemon curd by standing on my tippy-toes, wearing my very own little apron, on a step stool stirring. I have lots of amazing memories attached to food.

I grew up in a beautiful small town called Lake County. It is about 1.5 hours outside of Napa Valley, CA. Fabulous, gourmet food was literally at my fingertips from the beginning.

The combination of stellar home cooking and phenomenal restaurant choices encouraged the inner-foodie in me.

Food as Fuel

Food became a bit of a crutch. When it was time to celebrate, I turned to food. When I was sad, I turned to food. When I was bored, I turned to food. So hunger was not necessarily the trigger for eating. My issue at the time was that I didn't understand the concept of good calories versus empty calories. I also wasn't thinking about food as "fuel" for my body. Food was more like an answer for dealing with my emotions.

Knowing this now doesn't mean I don't enjoy my food. It simply means that I am aware of the direct correlation between the types of food I put in my body and how my choices make me feel. When I started this program, I went to that nutritionist in Loomis. The bottom line is WHOLE CLEAN FOODS are what you should fuel your body with. So I came up with a few rules that I followed diligently in my 90 day journey.

Rachel's L2F90 Eating Tips
Eat every 2 hours
Drink water!
No fried foods
No cream sauces
No white flour, sugar, or processed foods
Eat veggies at almost every meal (you can't "over veggie")
Limit fruit and stop eating it by 3:00 p.m.
No fake sugar
Eat lean meats
Last meal by 8:00 p.m.

A great rule of thumb is to stick to the outside aisle of the grocery store. This is where you'll find the fresh produce, as well as the meat and fish counters. How simple is that?

> To eat healthy, stick to the outside perimeter of the grocery store for your proteins, fresh veggies, and fruit.

If you follow this rule, you'll be able to avoid all of the processed foods in the center aisles that have refined sugar, an abundance of salt, and white flour. These are normally the big temptations! Now don't get me wrong, I LOVE having a treat but I'm not going to indulge in my temptations every day of the week. I now abide by an "85/15 rule." I eat well 85% of the time, and 15% of the time I have that piece of bread or chocolate cake!

Redefine Cheating

I have heard people talk about "cheat days" and I have a lot to say about that now that I have a new understanding of food. My first thought is why call it a cheat day, when it should really be referring to a single meal off of your program? There's a big misconception that if you indulge in one unhealthy meal or snack, you have messed up your whole day… so you might as well eat whatever you crave that entire day. This is actually perfectionism at its worst and it can really defeat your attempts at transforming your life. It's all about calories. You can easily have a treat now, and finish the rest of your day strong. There is no need to throw out your entire day over a brownie – which is something I used to do.

In addition, it is a good practice to avoid the idea that you are "cheating." You aren't cheating. You are developing a new lifestyle and a way of treating your body and eating well! On a day you decide to eat a cheeseburger, it is simply a splurge from your normal kind of eating routine. It is OK to treat yourself now and then. You deserve it. It's in your 85/15!

Embrace the 85/15 rule!

It is also important to monitor your feelings of hunger. Often when we reach for food, our bodies are actually crying out for water. It is quite common for people to mistake their thirst for hunger. (Says the NOW water expert!)

Another thing I have implemented that has really changed my life is to stop eating after 8:00 p.m. If I get hungry after that, I chug a glass of water. Nine times out of ten, I am simply dehydrated.

Develop Your Inner Guidance System

The good news is, the longer you eat clean and treat your body well, the more you get to know it. You will develop your inner guidance system and know when you are eating something that doesn't agree with your body and isn't good for you. Your body is always talking to you and giving you signs for what it wants; the question is, are you listening?

Nina's Knowledge: Your Nutrition and Fuel

It is estimated that Americans spend about 42 billion dollars on nutrition and weight loss programs. The numbers are astonishing and the results are abysmal! My experience working with countless clients has been that long-term healthy eating and weight loss doesn't result from popular diets and programs.

So if you have had experiences with diets, diet programs, diet books, diet food, diet supplements, diet drugs, etc. you may have cluttered and confused your mind with a ton of conflicting information. The more diet programs and products you have used or participated in, the more you may be confused. Creating a healthy lifestyle is actually quite straightforward. So let's start with your relationship with food.

Your Relationship with Food

When I was in college I lifted a lot of weights and was really focused on being lean and building muscle. I had a friend who won the bodybuilding title "Mr. Texas" at that time. He told me something that stuck with me. Watch the person whose body you admire and do what they're doing. I took that advice and it has continued to aid me over the years. Because of this, I was able to workout 2.5 hours a day and change my eating habits to truly support my goals.

As a result, I changed my perception of food as well as my emotional connection to food. I would eat with the guys who I trained with and order what they did, just in smaller portions. Eating with a group of bodybuilders was interesting. Connecting food choices with my goals was completely new to me and yet it was fundamental for building muscle and staying lean.

I found myself looking forward to my "Junior Lumberjack" breakfast. It had 9 egg whites, half a chicken breast, broccoli, and a sweet potato (the guys had 15 egg whites and a whole chicken breast)! Needless to say, I didn't feel deprived missing the French toast breakfast that had always been my favorite. I found my relationship with food changed when I really began to understand that everything I put in my mouth was either helping me reach my goals or keeping me from my goals. Food became fuel first and foremost.

I continued to use and expand on the advice I was given. I'd watch a person that I admired and do what they did. This really worked wonders on my love for sweets. I used to eat out with a group of girlfriends and we'd often share a dessert. One of my friends didn't care about sweets at all. One day I decided to follow her lead. I would only take a bite of our shared dessert if she did. To my sweet tooth's heartbreak, she would usually take two bites total and then put her fork down. So I begrudgingly started to do the same. While I ate my two measly bites, I became aware of the inner dialogue that had always pushed me to keep eating. Paying attention to that inner dialogue was the key to changing my ways with sugar permanently.

Once my relationship with food changed, I became interested in observing other people's relationships with food. After years of observing those who exercised discipline and control over their food choices, it became apparent that they had a logical connection to food. Food was their fuel, not their comfort. They still enjoyed it but without the emotional attachment. This allowed them to make healthy choices. So truly understanding the components of your emotional connection with food is instrumental for your success.

What to Eat

Focus on lean proteins and complex carbohydrates (lots of veggies) What you put in your body not only impacts your health but also has the potential to enhance the benefits of your exercise program. Healthy food choices increase your concentration power and will help you function at your best. Your improved relationship with food will support your optimal health. Shifting the focus on what to eat rather than what to cut out will keep you more motivated and on track.

Types of Fuel

Complete Proteins: These proteins contain 9 amino acids. They build, maintain, and repair tissues in your body. Lean proteins such as chicken, fish, and very lean red meat are your best choices for weight loss or building and maintaining muscle. If you are a vegetarian, you will need to combine your proteins in order to make the complete 9 amino acids (such as lentils with whole grain bread). See the website for information about combining proteins.

Carbohydrates: Naturally occurring carbohydrates include: fruit, milk, nuts, grains, seeds, legumes, and vegetables. Starch and sugar also fall in this category. This provides your "running around fuel."

Complex Fibrous Carbohydrates: These are made up of multiple sugar units bonded together. Most of your vegetables, grains, beans, and peas are complex carbohydrates. Typically, complex carbohydrates contain fiber, vitamins, and nutrients.

Simple Carbohydrates: Sugar is the simplest form of carbohydrate. It occurs naturally in foods like fruits (fructose), vegetables, milk, and dairy products (lactose).

Types of Sugars

Learn all the names of sugars.

- **Granular:** white, brown, raw, coconut, powdered, etc.
- **Liquid sugars:** sodas, juices, fruit drinks, etc.
- **Syrups:** corn, rice, maple, honey, agave, molasses, etc.
- **Sugar alcohols:** sorbitol, mannitol, xylitol, isomalt, and hydrogenated starch hydrolysates (plant products altered through a chemical process). These may have fewer calories, but their artificial sweetness often contributes to increased sugar cravings.

Note: The label "sugar free" often increases the amount people will consume.

Fats

Fats: There are two essential fatty acids (EFA's): alpha-linoleic acid (an omega-3 fatty acid) and linoleic acid (an omega-6 fatty acid). Fats are critical for the metabolic functions in the body.

Now we are going to go into a list of foods that I fuel my body with, and provide you with a list of optimal foods versus not so good foods.

> Be sure to check out our website and online community for lots of wonderful L2F90 recipes. We have a whole network of Lost to Founders sharing their favorites!

L2F90 Clean Eating Grocery List

Proteins

- [ ] chicken breast
- [ ] turkey breast
- [ ] turkey ham
- [ ] tuna
- [ ] halibut
- [ ] tuna steaks
- [ ] sole
- [ ] grouper
- [ ] lean beef
- [ ] orange ruffy
- [ ] cheese
- [ ] venison
- [ ] red snapper
- [ ] salmon
- [ ] non-fat tofu
- [ ] protein pasta
- [ ] quinoa
- [ ] low/no fat tofu
- [ ] veggie meat substitutes
- [ ] almonds or walnuts – *small amount 6-12*

Veggies (aka Fibrous Carbs)

- [ ] asparagus
- [ ] green beans
- [ ] zucchini
- [ ] squash
- [ ] celery
- [ ] broccoli
- [ ] watercress
- [ ] cauliflower
- [ ] cucumbers
- [ ] mushrooms
- [ ] green or red peppers
- [ ] spinach
- [ ] collards
- [ ] salsa
- [ ] green chile
- [ ] turnips
- [ ] eggplant
- [ ] artichokes
- [ ] beets
- [ ] iceberg lettuce
- [ ] brussel sprouts
- [ ] cabbage
- [ ] romaine
- [ ] tomatoes
- [ ] onions
- [ ] kale

Complex Carbs

- [ ] corn
- [ ] mushrooms
- [ ] yams
- [ ] corn tortillas
- [ ] cream of rice cereal
- [ ] brown rice
- [ ] peas
- [ ] pinto beans
- [ ] black beans
- [ ] air popped popcorn
- [ ] carrots
- [ ] sweet potatoes
- [ ] grits
- [ ] lentils
- [ ] fat free refried beans
- [ ] whole wheat pasta
- [ ] steelcut oatmeal

Fruits

- [ ] apples
- [ ] bananas
- [ ] blueberries
- [ ] strawberries
- [ ] blackberries
- [ ] oranges
- [ ] grapes
- [ ] grapefruit
- [ ] pomegranate
- [ ] pineapple
- [ ] raspberries
- [ ] cherries
- [ ] kiwis
- [ ] coconuts
- [ ] cantaloupe
- [ ] mango
- [ ] passion fruit
- [ ] honeydew
- [ ] papaya
- [ ] avocado (also a good fat)

Oils

- [ ] olive oil
- [ ] coconut oil
- [ ] avocado oil
- [ ] walnut oil
- [ ] grapeseed oil

Nuts & Seeds

- [ ] almonds
- [ ] flax seeds
- [ ] hemp
- [ ] sunflower seeds
- [ ] cashews
- [ ] peanuts
- [ ] nut butters
- [ ] pumpkin seeds

Flours

- [ ] oat
- [ ] chickpea
- [ ] spelt
- [ ] coconut
- [ ] almond
- [ ] rice
- [ ] wheat

How to Eat

"No-Brainer" Meal

Create breakfast, lunch, and dinner meals that are simple to prepare. Have the ingredients on your weekly shopping list so that they are available. Align your food with your goals. The primary components of your meals should be a lean protein with a serving of vegetables.

Examples:
Chicken stir-fry with veggies
Egg frittata: egg whites, spinach, tomatoes, and asparagus
Tilapia with veggies
Ground turkey lettuce wraps

"Tokens" for the week: These fall into your 15% category. Limit the number of times you eat unhealthy snacks but when you do, do it consciously and enjoy your "break." If you are trying to really reduce your weight, limit your tokens to 1-2 per week. Use your tokens freely, without guilt, on foods or alcohol. Don't blow your tokens on something you don't really love, be selective, and choose wisely (for example, bypass the office birthday cake for the bread pudding dessert at your favorite restaurant.)

If you are at the stage where you are maintaining your current weight, continue to use tokens to establish a limit on your treats. This will help you maintain your weight. The number of tokens you get per week will vary depending on the number and kind of workouts you do.

Find a New Direction: Analyze Your Relationship with Food

Answer the following questions:

Food Self-Analysis – Part 1
How do you know when you are hungry? What do you feel? What happens in your body?
Do you feel full? How do you know when you are full?
Are you aware of foods that give you energy or foods that make you tired?
On a scale of 1-10, how much do you like food?
On a scale of 1-10, how important is what you eat for each meal?

Food Self-Analysis – Part 2

What are your favorite things to eat?

Do you get to eat them often or when you want?

Do you feel like others get to eat more than you do?

Do you believe others get to eat what they want?

Have you deprived yourself of food or certain types of food?

If so, what are the foods you have deprived yourself?

Do you feel food is a reward?

Do you believe you deserve to be able to eat certain foods? What are they?

Food Self-Analysis – Part 3

Do you eat when you are anxious, bored, or sad?

How important is food as a part of a celebration?

What do you do after you eat a meal?

What were your mealtimes like growing up?

Do you have special memories of moments and holidays that involve food?

Is there someone in your life that showed their love by cooking your favorite meals?

Are you the person that shares love with others by cooking, baking, or making their favorite foods?

Review and analyze your responses.

- What do your answers tell you about your relationship with food?
- Do you feel you have power over your food choices regularly?
- What else do you notice about your answers?
- Do you see any patterns?
- Is there anything that surprises you?
- Do you feel like you have a comprehensive understanding about your relationship with food now?

Diet is what you eat, not something you are on. Everything you put in your mouth is either supporting your goals or sabotaging them. Focus on the foods that support your goals.

Weekly Commitment

Your Activity

1. Write and sign a commitment about food and share it with your accountability partner/ L2F90 Community.

2. Create an affirmation that reminds you that food is your fuel and supports your goals. Have that affirmation available to see, read, and say aloud throughout the day.

3. What do you feel like you need to be successful in order to make healthy food

4. Create 10 meal options with a lean protein and vegetables:
   - Lean protein _____ and Veggies _____
   - Lean protein _____ and Veggies _____
   - Lean protein _____ and Veggies _____
   - Lean protein _____ and Veggies _____
   - Lean protein _____ and Veggies _____
   - Lean protein _____ and Veggies _____
   - Lean protein _____ and Veggies _____
   - Lean protein _____ and Veggies _____
   - Lean protein _____ and Veggies _____
   - Lean protein _____ and Veggies _____

5. Make a basic grocery list from these meals below:

Your Grocery List
1.
2.
3.
4.
5.
6.
7.
8.
9.
10.

6. Keep a food log. Knowledge is power. To gain awareness of your choices, track them below:

Meal	MON	TUES	WED	THUR	FRI	SAT	SUN
Breakfast							
Snack							
Lunch							
Snack							
Dinner							
Snack							

    a. Identify your lean proteins and vegetables with a circle.
    b. Star your "tokens"
    c. What are the things that are not circled?
    d. Did you have 1-2 Stars?

> **Your Accountability:** Connect with your accountability partner and share your 10 protein and veggie meals, and your grocery list for the week

Your Journal

Journal about your answers to the questions in this chapter to help you understand more about the role food has played in your life.

- What is the impact food has played on your life?
- What do you want to do differently?
- What do you need to be successful?

There are often multiple reasons for the food habits you've developed. Knowing how your history has influenced the way you relate to food and your food choices is extremely important. Use your journal to capture your feelings, thoughts, observations, and "Aha" moments regarding the above.

- BSE – Body Status Exam – Check in with how your body is feeling.
- MSE – Mental Status Exam – Check in with what you are thinking.

Your Thoughts and Notes:

Lost to Found in 90 Days: Chapter 5

Chapter 6:
Your Exercise and Sleep

Rachel's Journey

I've always been drawn to the next new thing that promises to give me results… and if that thing happens to give me abs like Beyoncé, more power to it!

However, this has produced piles of unopened workout DVDs, the most recent abdominal roller from a late night infomercial, several workout stretch bands, and even a "shake weight" (don't judge, it was bought in a weak moment…who can turn down two for the price of one?!). I seem to always be looking for the next best thing.

When I decided to commit myself to these 90 days of transformation, I needed something consistent that wasn't too difficult. I started simple. Every morning when I woke up, I would drink a glass of water, and drop to the floor to do 25 squats, 45 crunches, and 22 pushups. There was no rhyme or reason to those numbers except for the fact that I wanted to get this done in ten minutes, and it would wake me up. This wasn't easy in the beginning but I was deeply committed. And so my journey began.

Before and After

I decided to take photos of myself every 30 days. I knew I wasn't going to love my before pictures but I was determined to see a difference. I cannot emphasize the importance of this process. I heard a great saying that really rang true for me. "It takes 4 weeks for you to notice a difference, 8 weeks for your friends, and 12 weeks for everyone else." How convenient that this works out to be just over a 12 week program!

It takes 4 weeks for you to notice a difference, 8 weeks for your friends, and 12 weeks for everyone else.

A funny thing started to happen as I committed to my new way of eating and morning exercise routine, I started to feel better. The first thing that I noticed was that I was no longer bloated. The second thing I noticed was that I had to pee every 5 minutes from all the water I was drinking!

At about 4 weeks into my program I felt like my nutrition was on point, my water was regulated, and my morning routine was no longer a huge effort. At this point I made the decision to increase my workout routine. It's easier to build on small successes rather than set yourself up for failure by taking on too much at once.

The 10K

I have always wanted to be a runner. I was told about this effective app for your cell phone called the 10k. It's a great app that allows you to play your favorite music (I use Pandora) while it builds on itself and eventually gets you to run a solid 10 kilometers. It directs you to switch from walking to jogging every minute and a half. Eventually, you are running more than you are walking, and within no time you're a

runner. I finally understood a "runner's high!" I felt like I deserved a t-shirt.
At about week 8, I was running 3 days a week and lifting light weights. Weight lifting was always scary to me. I didn't want to bulk up. As I've mentioned, I am only 5 feet tall and the last time I tried lifting weights, I ended up looking like a mini-hulk. That's not sexy!

So this time, I worked out with a trainer and combined weight lifting with body resistance exercises. I did the combined routines with a 30 second interval between "supersets." At this point, my body started to change! I was losing body fat, losing inches, and gaining muscle! The compliments started to roll in, and it made me want more!

Find Your Flow

Closer to week 12, I also added in Vinyasa Flow Yoga. I was feeling pretty good about myself but wanted to be able to really unwind from the day. Vinyasa Flow is a type of yoga where you do several movements to stretch and elongate your muscles. You work on correct body positioning and sweat your butt off (the room is literally 106 degrees)!

I was finally treating my body like a temple, feeding it good food, hydrating it regularly, and sweating out the stress! Life was feeling good!

Sleep On It

Now let's chat about sleep or in my case, the lack thereof. If any of you follow me on Facebook, you know it was common to see me posting at 2:00 a.m. Insomnia and I had become good buddies. I actually started having sleep issues back in 2007, and to combat this, I took sleeping pills. I had taken them four days a week for the last seven years. I was also using Advil extensively for headaches.

This is how my sleep routine went:

- Get home between 8:00-9:00 p.m.
- Eat dinner.
- Sit on my couch and watch TV or keep working with a glass of wine or tea.
- Venture to bed around midnight.
- Whip out my cell phone (which was never more than two feet away from me) and check my emails one more time.
- Then look through all my social media feeds to "unwind" from my day. This entailed Facebook, Instagram, E! Online, Twitter, and People Magazine. In my head, I was relaxing! In reality, I was revving up my mind and increasing stress and mental fatigue.
- So rather than drifting off to sleep, my thoughts zoomed from: "Oh... I want that dress!" to "Whoa, is he really dating her?" to "OMG, stop posting about you and your boyfriend fighting!" to "I wonder if that comes in my size?" Yes... that was me unwinding!!
- Between 2:00-3:00 a.m., I would finally fall asleep.

I remember talking to Nina about my sleep issue. She, of course, asked me about myroutine. It wasn't rocket science that my routine was affecting my sleep. I was exhausted every morning, and by 3:00 p.m. I was reaching for coffee and ready for a nap!

Seek Your Sanctuary

Nina explained to me that my bedroom should be a sanctuary, not another work station. She told me to create a spa-like environment. We created some rules for me to follow:

1. No cell phone use in the bedroom. I was allowed to check my emails and social media one hour before bed, in a different part of the house, but I had to leave my phone outside my bedroom.

2. Get a sound machine. Often white noise, such as raindrops or ocean waves, can quiet the mind.

3. Use calming essential oils such as lavender and drink calming teas such as chamomile.

4. Dim lights a half hour before bedtime. Once I got into bed, there was no reading. It was lights out.
5. Learn to love the quiet in my head. This was a struggle, since I'm always on the go, so Nina introduced me to guided meditation CD's. (You can also find some great ones on YouTube.) These provided a great tool for ensuring restful sleep.

The Power of Intention

I also learned the power of intention. Say I only had 6 hours to sleep. If my thought around this was, "Oh shoot, I only have 6 hours to sleep. I'm going to wake up exhausted," then that is exactly what would happen. However, if I changed my approach to, "Ok I have 6 hours to get the best and most restful sleep possible. I am going to relax my mind, embrace deep breathing, and wake up refreshed," then that is exactly what would happen! Your mindset is a powerful thing. It can positively or negatively affect your outcomes, so make sure your mindset is positive! A negative thinker sees difficulty in every situation. A positive thinker sees an opportunity in every difficulty.

> *A negative thinker sees difficulty in every situation. A positive thinker sees an opportunity in every difficulty.*

Following Nina's rules for sleep has changed my life! It doesn't mean that I always sleep perfectly but it has improved markedly.

Nina's Knowledge: Sleep and Exercise

Sleep

Sleep is one of the foundations of good health. Lack of sleep is becoming more and more common. In fact, the Center for Disease Control is now referring to sleep problems as a "public epidemic."

According to the CDC, 40% of people in the U.S. do not get the recommended seven to nine hours needed to support proper health functions (children and teenagers need even more.) What this means is that almost half of the population in our country is not getting the required amount of sleep to support their bodies.

The Results of Insufficient Sleep

People with less sleep generally spend more time at the doctor, and on healthcare in general, than those that are well rested.

- A chronic lack of sleep increases your potential to suffer from migraines and headaches.
- Studies verify that you are also three times more likely to catch a cold virus when you regularly get fewer than seven hours of sleep per night.
- Lack of sleep makes you more sensitive to pain.
- Research has shown that sleeping five hours or less a night has been associated with a 45% increase in the risk for heart attacks.
- Keeping people awake also increases their blood pressure. In one study, a group of young, healthy males were tested after one bad night of sleep (3.6 hours). There were significant temporary changes in their blood pressure.

Results of Insufficient Sleep
Negative moods
Mental health: People who sleep less tend to battle more depression, anxiety, and lower self-esteem
Chronic skin conditions
Reduced libido
Reduced ability to build muscle and repair cells

Results of Insufficient Sleep
Reduced ability to control blood sugar and increased risk of diabetes
Accelerated aging
Weakened immune system
Decreased pain threshold

Do you want fewer mistakes?
Sleep!

Not only will you make fewer mistakes when you get enough sleep but you actually will make fewer dangerous mistakes. In 2003, the medical profession began to regulate the number of hours a resident could work. This occurred after a Harvard study found that reducing a doctor's hours from an 80+ hour week to a 63 hour week, caused residents to make fewer serious medical errors. The more sleep-deprived group made 22% more serious errors.

Famous accidents like the Space Shuttle Challenger explosion and the Exxon Valdez oil spill have been attributed, at least in part, to mistakes made by people with sleep deprivation. Sleep-deprived workers in general, are much more likely to have dangerous accidents. One study involving 50,000 people in Sweden, found that a lack of sleep made people twice as likely to die in an accident.

Look at Your Sleep

Too often people aren't aware of their sleeping patterns. Sleep impacts every area of your health and your life. It is a fundamental building block for establishing good health.

What Are Your Specific Sleep Needs?

What happens when you get enough sleep, compared to when you don't?

- Does sleep affect your energy level or your mood?
- Do you notice issues with your digestion or weight?
- Do you notice an impact on your decision-making ability, learning ability, creativity, or problem solving skills?

Your Sleep Needs
What time do you go to bed during the week?
What is your sleep environment like?
What are your challenges for getting a good night's sleep?
What are your tools to help you sleep (sounds, lighting, fragrances, technology, etc.)?
When and where were you when you got your best sleep? What were the circumstances? Envision a good night's sleep and describe your circumstances.
Reduced libido
Reduced ability to build muscle and repair cells
Reduced ability to control blood sugar and increased risk of diabetes
Accelerated aging
Weakened immune system
Decreased pain threshold

Keep a Log

Keep a log of what you do each evening. This will help you better understand the events leading to a good or bad night's sleep.

Document Your Evening		
Time	What Are You Doing?	Thoughts
5:00 p.m.		
6:00 p.m.		
7:00 p.m.		
8:00 p.m.		
9:00 p.m.		
10:00 p.m.		

Document Your Evening		
Time	**What Are You Doing?**	**Thoughts**
11:00 p.m.		
12:00 a.m.		
1:00 a.m.		

Analyze Your Sleep
What do you notice about your time log?
What time do you stop eating before you go to bed? Going to bed on a full stomach puts a burden on the body digesting food.
What time do you go to bed?
What is the last thing that you do before you fall asleep?
Do you notice any patterns in your nightly activities?
Is sleep a problem for you?
Have you tried to address the challenges that you have with sleep? If so, how?
If you have had chronic sleep issues, have you tried a sleep study? (If you aren't able to sleep soundly and have never had a sleep study, do that immediately.)

Exercise

The topic of exercise can be confusing and complicated. There is a proliferation of conflicting information out there. It can also be emotionally challenging if you've had negative experiences in this area. So let's go to the powerful mindset of NO JUDGMENT.

Your Past, Present, and Future with Exercise

We need to treat everything we've done in the past as information that will help us move forward with our goals. The start of our journey is NOW. Our past simply arms us with useful knowledge. Keeping this in mind, let's look at our experiences to see what we can learn, in order to determine the best route for success.

The Past

Your Past Experience With Exercise
Think about what forms of exercise you've done in the past. Is there anything that you enjoyed doing or were able to consistently keep up?
Do you remember particular exercises that you've done in the past?
If you stopped those exercises, why?
If you continued them, why?

The Present

Your Present Experience With Exercise
What kind of exercise (if any) are you doing currently?
How do you feel when you're exercising?
How does your body feel after you exercise?
If you're not exercising, how do you feel physically?
Is there anything else you notice regarding your exercise routine or lack thereof?

The Future

Your Future Experience With Exercise
Is there any kind of exercise that interests you but you haven't had a chance to try it yet?
Is there any kind of exercise that you wish you could do but don't think you can?

Exercise Keys to Success

The three components to a balanced exercise program include strength training, cardio training, and flexibility training. The common error is to pick something from one or two of these categories, rather than all three. For example, if you enjoy running and lifting weights, it's common to focus your time on these activities. You may lack flexibility, so you avoid this component and avoid yoga or anything akin to it. That missing component, flexibility, actually impacts your overall health potential.

In order to be able to accomplish your health goals, you'll need an effective exercise program that contains all three of these components. Each component plays a vital part in your overall health and will make your exercise routine more efficient and effective.

Cardiovascular exercise is well known to support your heart health, burn calories, and aid in weight loss. There are so many varieties of cardiovascular exercise to choose from but you must commit to doing one of them. The key to effective cardio is understanding your goal and structuring your exercise to accomplish that goal.

Incremental Changes Make a Difference

Creating an exercise discipline takes practice and understanding. In my 20+ years working with clients, I can tell you that one of the most effective long-term weight loss methods is simply to walk 4 miles (6.4 kilometers) every day.

Walk It Out

There are two reasons why this approach is extremely beneficial. Walking 4 miles in about an hour is an effective, fat burning pace. The second is being able to feel good about your commitment of walking every day. Participating in an ongoing, scheduled appointment with yourself to walk validates your commitment to your health. With each walk, each day, you become stronger in your resolve to take care of yourself and to reach your goals.

The combination of walking, the time put into walking, and the continued commitment, results in building your personal power. As your body changes, your mind is more likely to change. When the two change together, it results in real, long-term, positive-lifestyle changes.

The Regenerative Effects of Weight Training

Muscles support our posture. Without strong muscles we wind up with multiple problems that poor body alignment creates. We also need strength and resistance training to keep our muscles strong. Doing resistance exercises slows down the aging process by keeping our muscles strong and toned, which dramatically affects the quality of our lives. A bonus of muscle tone is the visual benefits that come along with it!

Weight training fuels a regenerative state of growing and building muscle. This affects your body composition and shape, while also impacting your metabolic capacity. Without strength and resistance exercises, you can lose approximately 7/10 of a pound of muscle each year after the age of 29. A sedentary lifestyle increases this amount. 7/10 of a pound of muscle loss each year adds up. In 10 years, that's approximately 7 lbs. of muscle!

Why is this really concerning? Muscle burns more calories than fat. A pound of muscle burns approximately 50 more calories than a pound of fat. Not knowing why you can't eat the same amount of food you used to without gaining weight is a common theme for people. Now you know the reason. We need to keep up our muscle mass and metabolic rate in order to avoid weight gain as we age. Lifting weights or doing other resistance training is an effective key to maintaining a powerful body. It improves your health and gives you the added benefit of being able to keep up your fat burning power.

Stay Flexible

Flexibility is the third component of a balanced exercise regimen. It is also the component that often prevents everyday injuries, supports posture, increases athletic performance, and gives you a long, lean look. As our bodies age, they become more compressed and rigid. It is extremely important to stretch daily in order to prevent this painful and limiting aging process.

Flexibility is what I call the BONUS component because it also increases the benefits of cardio and strength training. Increased flexibility allows for more muscle fibers to be available for cardio and strength training.

Doing flexibility exercises throughout the day assists you in avoiding injuries, especially repetitive movement injuries. These are the most common injuries that I work on with clients. They are the injuries that occur from doing the same movements over and over on a continuous basis and almost everyone has had them. For example, the majority of knee injuries that I have helped clients with are caused by sitting at desks for long periods of time, which result in tight hip flexors.

When the hips are tight, the ball and socket of the hip joint has limited ability to rotate. If you find yourself in a situation in which your leg needs to rotate but your hip is tight, your leg will then try to twist at the knee. Twisting the knee forces ligaments and tendons to be overexerted and possibly tear.

These types of injuries can occur while performing daily activities. For this reason it's important to gain awareness about the state of your muscles. Scan your body to see what muscle groups are tight and feeling pain. Your first intervention and solution should be to stretch the areas that feel tight, in order to increase your range of motion and decrease the pain that accompanies tight muscles. Extremely tight muscles can actually pull bones out of alignment. This is why it is so important to stay flexible throughout our lives.

Find a New Direction: Your body

Below is a list of options that might interest you.

Strength Exercises	Flexibility	Cardio	Classes
Free-weights	Yoga	Walk	Jazzercise
Kettle Bells	Pilates	Jog	Zumba
Plyometrics	Assisted Stretching	Swim	Aerobics
Cross-training	Passive Stretching	Jump Rope	Cross Fit
Rock Climbing		Stair Stepper	Kickboxing
Body Weight Exercises			Spin

In the charts below, fill in examples of things you've done in the past, things you're currently doing, and things you'd like to do in the future. Make a note about what you've liked and disliked about each!

Exercise	Strength	Likes/Dislikes
Past		
Present		
Future		

Exercise	Flexibility	Likes/Dislikes
Past		
Present		
Future		

Exercise	Cardio	Likes/Dislikes
Past		
Present		
Future		

Your Weekly Commitment

Create solutions to meet your needs:

- Find an accountability partner/member of the L2F90 community
- Create and follow routines for exercise and sleeping that you share with your partner).
- Create a weekly schedule that includes work, exercise, family time, entertainment, and sleep.
- Sign a weekly commitment to your goals that keeps you accountable and on target.
- Establish a consistent bedtime and wake time.
- Use the checklist below to guide your accountability.

Your Weekly Checklist	
Do cardio 5-6 times per week	
Do strength training 2 - 3 times per week.	
Do flexibility 1 class or practice per week, plus additional stretching throughout the day.	
Schedule 7 - 8 hours of sleep per night and stick to it.	
Create your sleep environment.	
Power off technology at bedtime.	
Go to bed the same time every day.	
Use tools to help you wind down (relaxing music, essential oils, herbal tea, etc.).	
Sleep.	

> **Your Accountability:** Connect with your
> accountability partner to exchange checklists

Your Journal

Document how you feel and any observations you make as you begin to incorporate your new practices into your life.

Using your accountability partner, share the time you have agreed to schedule for journaling.

Review your goals throughout the journaling process.

- Review your journaling from the beginning.
- Note your observations about your successes, your goals, your changes, and anything that you want to do differently.
- Sign a weekly commitment to your goals that keeps you accountable.
- BSE – Body Status Exam – Check in with how your body is feeling.
- MSE – Mental Status Exam – Check in with what you are thinking.

Your Thoughts and Notes:

Chapter 7:
Your Mindset and Body Posture

Rachel's Journey

Mind Discipline 101

I have always been a "glass is half full" kind of woman. I always look for the bright side of any situation. I usually wake up in a good mood, ready to tackle the day. When I first got into real estate, I learned about the power of positive affirmations, and this further enhanced my outlook. I took a course called BOLD and learned, in depth, how to utilize and harness the power of positive affirmations.

Prior to this course, I lived my life dreaming about the kind of person I wanted to become and made a lot of "if/then" statements mentally and aloud. For example,

"If I work really hard, then I'll be a top producing agent." Another example is, "If I work out five days a week, then I'll finally be proud of my body." My mindset really shifted when I learned how to phrase positive affirmations correctly in order to realize them. The "if/then" phrasing completely left my vocabulary. I had no idea it was self-defeating!

I've mentioned before that it is really important to know what you want out of life and to create goals in order to achieve your dreams. Things really started to shift for me when I added talking about WHO I wanted to become, in addition to what I wanted out of life.

Become the Person Who Lives the Life You Want

This is what I learned in the process of using positive affirmations: Forget what happened to you last year. Forget what happened to you last week, and stop holding on to what happened yesterday. If you want to *become* someone, you have to *believe* you are already that person living the life you envision. You have to let go of the concept of who you have been, and replace it totally with who you want to become.

I took a look at the things in my life that I wanted to achieve and I wrote them down. Then I took a careful look at my wording. The words we use are extremely powerful so we have to use words with conscious intent.

> The words we use are extremely **powerful.**
> Use words consciously to harness their power and intent.

Turn Off the Negative Programming

From a young age, we are bombarded with negative phrasing. Think about some of the first words children learn. What are they? *"No!"* and *"Don't!"* So from the time we are young, we are used to negative programming. As adults, we have to learn new habits and new ways of thinking in order to escape negative outcomes.

When I got really clear on who I wanted to become, I became focused on how I communicated to others and myself. I also paid attention to the people I surrounded myself with, and even the kind of music I listened to. I realized how important it was that these things lined up with *who* I wanted to become.

I sat down to write a comprehensive list of the things that needed improvement in my life. When my list was completed, I took each item and turned it into a powerful sentence about the kind of person I wanted to become. The task was to turn them into statements that affirmed that I had already achieved this state of being. *Remember, you must write and speak affirmations as if you are already that person.*

Harness the Power

Once I had my affirmations completed, I went to work harnessing their power. You must repeat your affirmations throughout the day. I typed mine out ten times and then printed them. To keep them on my mind, I hung them all over the place… my office, my car, my bathroom mirror, and even my front door! The point was, if I wanted to become that person, I was going to have to walk my talk! Here's an example of one of the areas I wanted to tackle.

My original statement was:
"I wish I liked my body more… I am dehydrated and I don't feel good."

And this is how I flipped it into a positive affirmation on who I wanted to become:
"I eat clean. I am tight, toned, and drink a gallon of water a day. I feel great!"

To ensure my success, I took this practice one step further by asking my best friend and business partner, Matt, to be my accountability partner. Every morning at 8:00 a.m., we would call each other and share our affirmations aloud. After we said them to one another, we would encourage one another by validating them. It felt so powerful and amazing. And guess what? After a while, my list of affirmations started to come true! I had transformed my old beliefs about myself and was exemplifying the person I affirmed daily. What we think is a powerful thing!

Who Do You Want to Become?

I love Henry Ford's quote: *"Whether you think you can or you think you can't – you're right."* So now I say to you, it's entirely up to you. You can do this. Who do you want to become? It's time to exercise your power to use your voice consciously and live the life you want. Now it's your turn to create your positive affirmations.

Rachel's Affirmations

- *My toned and fit 130lb. body helps me achieve all of my dreams!*
- *I am in charge of how I feel and today I choose happiness!*
- *I am a great leader and I lead by example.*
- *I am a great listener and offer value to those around me.*

- *Every experience that I have is perfect for my growth.*
- *I live my best life with full integrity and heart.*
- *I am truly content with who I am and am ready for love.*
- *I get out of my own way and allow God to show me His path.*

Whether you think you can or you think you can't - you're right.

Fiction and Nonfiction

Once I began to make headway with my affirmations, I addressed a second component that affects mindset. Do you know that we all make up stories in our heads every day? Not only do we do this but these stories very often wreak havoc on our peace of mind. Let me give you an example:

You call your friend and she doesn't call you back. So, instead of giving her the benefit of the doubt, your mind makes up a story. "She must be mad at me." Then you spend precious time racking your brain, thinking about what you did to upset your friend. You drive yourself crazy, analyzing your last few conversations and just can't figure it out. Then you either get mad because you haven't done anything to deserve her anger or you wind up with a stomach ache because you never want to hurt anyone. Maybe you send a text message just to double-check. Again, there's no reply. "Yep, something is definitely wrong." You spend your afternoon stressing out. Your mind then wonders if there has been a tragic accident. "Maybe she is hurt? Gosh what is going on?"

Your story has now cost you hours of productivity and has left you feeling anxious, tired, and misunderstood. That's a whole lot of stress you really didn't need. Finally you get a text message, "Hey! Sorry for the delay. I misplaced my phone. How was your day?" You breathe a huge sigh of relief and rejoice over the fact that everything is OK. Looks like it was all just in your head.

How many times a week do we do this? This might be an exaggerated version of what occurs. However, the point is to demonstrate that when we allow our minds to spin, it produces a lot of self-doubt. Using positive affirmations helps tremendously. If you are always looking at life through solution-based lenses, you are focusing on the bright side of things. You see solutions and opportunities for growth, instead of problems. It is a beautiful way experience life.

Body Discipline 101

Now that you know how important your mindset is, let's chat about how important your body posture is. Holy moly, this one was totally new for me! At this point, my mindset was strong. I was working out regularly, eating healthy foods, sleeping better, and down a few pounds. I really felt on track. Overall I would say things had majorly improved. Then I flew down to see Nina to discuss creating this program. We went over how much had changed for me. She then began asking me questions...

Nina: "How do you feel?"

Rachel: "Really good!"

Nina: "How are you eating?"

Rachel: "Super healthy!"

Nina: "How does your body feel now?"

Rachel: "Better! I mean, I still get tired around 3:00 p.m. but overall I feel good."

Nina and I chatted for a while longer. We then went for a walk on the beach and had a healthy lunch back at her house. After feeding our hearts with cardiovascular exercise, our bodies with good nutrition, and our souls with great conversation, we began to talk about my workout routine. For years, I have worked out in a gym – often with a trainer. Nina and I went downstairs to her garage where her home gym was located.

Tighten That Core

She first had me stand in correct body alignment. We began to talk about each exercise I did with my trainer. That hour spent with Nina was eye opening. She started with the basics. We went through lunges, squats, bar curls, pushups, sit-ups, and several other exercises. The craziest thing was that I was doing all of them improperly. So before I started each exercise, she made sure I was standing in proper body position and then she had me tighten my core. With a tight core *everything* was different! I found that when I was in the correct body position, my workout was much more effective. I was amazed. She taught me that by engaging my core, it would make the workouts more efficient which could allow me to do less reps. My busy lifestyle was happily onboard!

If you think about your body's core, you will realize that it not only holds you upright but it supports all of your movements. This, in turn, has significant effects

on your mindset. Yes, you heard me correctly. If you regularly slump over with shoulders curled, you are actually holding a defeated posture and your mind will follow this cue with a matching mindset. However, if you are standing erect with your shoulders back, supported by a strong core, you are holding a "power pose." This will also affect your mindset in a powerful way. So, strengthening your core can have remarkable outcomes. A strong core will make you literally shine with confidence!

I now think of my core as a support system for shaping my daily attitude. *"My strong, inner core helps me make good decisions, lead my life with integrity, and go after the life of my dreams."* And this is how my latest affirmation was born!

Stretch Goals

Nina also taught me the importance of stretching. Stretching is fundamental to a healthy workout, which is why she recommends it after every exercise.

Nina's Routine
1. Breathe/Get present
2. Stretch
3. Good body position
4. Lunges
5. Stretch
6. Deadlifts

Nina's Routine
7. Stretch
8. Curls
9. Stretch
10. Overhead press
11. Stretch
12. Counter push ups
13. Stretch

I returned home and went to the gym newly armed with knowledge. My mindset was strong, my body was feeling better, my clothes were fitting looser, and I was headed in the right direction. I felt like I had a new lease on life!

I Enjoy Long Walks on the Beach

Several weeks later, I flew back to San Diego to meet with Nina again. We discussed the positive changes that were taking place in my life. She was so proud of me. It felt good to be making progress and sticking to my goals. We talked about my journey and how much had changed for me. We decided to go for another walk on the beach. As we walked, Nina continued to coach me. We talked about how much my mindset had improved regarding my eating habits. We also discussed how much water I was drinking, how I was sleeping, and how I felt in general.

At this point I was feeling remarkably better. It was clear that I would complete my 90 days triumphantly. My preference for having a timeline-associated goal had made this program a great fit. It was one more sizable thing to strike off my Goals List! Then something entirely organic and surprising occurred. I was feeling so empowered with my new, healthy lifestyle, that I didn't want my 90 days to end. I couldn't believe that I wanted MORE! I realized I would not be going back to my old ways.

On that telling walk on the beach, Nina asked me, "Are you happy with your body now? I know you are getting lots of compliments, and it's clear others have noticed your hard work but are you happy?" I realized I was happier but I wouldn't say I was feeling "finished." There were still things I wanted to improve. When I shared this with her, she smiled and asked me to explain. "Well, I want to continue to lose more body fat, see more definition and feel even stronger."

Nina proceeded to take the next hour working with me on a new practice – proper walking posture. She made me aware that I was pitching forward while we walked on the beach. Nina explained to me that often people who are so driven in life, push forward in more ways than one. This group tends to make quick decisions, want to rush to the end goal, and even eats faster! She pointed out that this was why I was actually leaning forward as I walked! I was literally trying to plunge ahead in life with each step I took!

Strong to the Core

"Think of your powerful self," she said. "You are a strong woman who will make a difference in this world. Strong women are strong at their core. We are going to keep working on your core and train you to walk and stand upright. As we do, you will feel a shift in yourself. Your inner confidence will build alongside your core. I promise you, when you walk into a room, people will know you are there." Well that sounded good to me!

Here's how it began…

- Stand up straight.
- Bring shoulder blades toward each other and drop them down.
- Bring chest up
- Pull belly button toward your spine
- Don't lock knees

Try this and you'll understand what I experienced. I stood like this for a while. It felt uncomfortable. It felt new. However, as we began to walk, I realized I felt immediately different. I felt stronger. I did feel confident. It was a much more powerful body language and my mind understood this quickly. In addition, my back also hurt! Change can often be uncomfortable but the beautiful thing about discomfort is that it often brings growth. As I learned in BOLD, breakdowns produce breakthroughs!

*Breakdowns
Produce Breakthroughs.*

I was breaking down my old way of walking (and thinking!), and a more confident, empowered woman was emerging. We continued to work on my body posture.

I became aware that a strong core was the foundation for everything in my life.

As mentioned previously, a strong core has the power to make your workouts more effective. It can also make you less susceptible to injuries, make you more psychologically powerful in stressful situations, and produce a wellspring of inner strength. As my core began to strengthen, I started to feel like I could achieve anything. What an impact a strong core and good posture can make!

> Check out the **L2F90 Inspirational Guidance Video** this week to learn a great tip for getting a workout while you drive! *Six pack abs at the wheel? Yes please!*

Nina's Knowledge: Mindset and Body Posture

There are two practices that stand out in terms of achieving long-term health, "Healthy Mindset" and "Good Body Position." These labels are deceiving and may lead you to believe that both are simple, and yet the majority of my clients over the past two decades have struggled with these. A healthy mindset involves a good relationship between your thoughts and your body, while good body position involves (but is not limited to) maintaining the proper posture in everything you do. Essentially these practices allow you to get more work done in less time, with improved results.

So let's look at what occurs if our mind is inundated with negative thoughts about our body and/or our life. Our health and work will suffer and our goals will be next to impossible to reach. We cannot achieve success when we are constantly our own biggest enemy. We need to be our biggest ally.

Mixed Signals

If we have poor body position, we send all kinds of signals to our brain that hinder our performance. Some of these are psychological. For instance, if we are used to constrictive body language (i.e., hunched over/crestfallen), we send a message to our brain that we are defeated. As a result, our outcomes will reflect this message.

In addition, if our body position forces us to squeeze a particular group of muscles consistently, we will compress various organs and joints, and constrict blood flow to these areas. This will cause stagnation from poor circulation, and over time, can lead to pain, injury, and other health issues.

Your Mindset

To create a healthy mindset, you need to truly understand the status of your current mindset. In your weekly L2F90 Chronicles, you have had the opportunity to gather detailed information about yourself. Your Mental Status Exam (MSE) should be revealing how you're thinking and feeling, as well as your perception of yourself. Your Body Status Exam (BSE) should be making you aware of how your body feels and operates, as well as how you are changing in general. Now that you have a detailed look at yourself over time, you have the information that will remove the blocks to achieving your healthy mindset.

The Waking Up & Becoming Aware Exercise is meant to bring you even more detailed information that will help your journey.

Answer the following questions with as much detail as possible:

Your Self-Talk
What have you been told and what do you think about... • ... how you look? • ... your body? • ... parts of your body? • ... who you are? • ... your character? • ... your skills and abilities? • ... what you are doing?
What do you say to yourself (in your head or aloud) when you are in front of a mirror getting ready to go out? Trying on new clothes? Trying on bathing suits?
Do you share your weight or size openly if anyone asks?
Do you have any nicknames? How do those nicknames make you feel?
Do you have any body parts that you refer to by nickname? What are those nicknames?
What are the phrases you use when you talk about how you look in clothes?
What are the phrases you use when you talk about how you look naked?
Do you read any health or fitness magazines?
What are your thoughts and feelings when you see photos of models and celebrities? Do you compare yourself to them?
What have you been told or keep telling your body?

Reflect on your answers:

- When you look at your answers do you notice anything in particular?
- Are there any patterns?
- What do you think about your answers?
- Is there anything that you feel like doing differently because of your answers?
- How do you feel after finishing this exercise?

Talk nicely to your body – **It hears you!**

Arm Yourself with Information

If you want a child to do well in school, would you tell them they are stupid? No, you would encourage them so that they would be open to learning. You want a child to feel good because this will affect his or her outcome in a positive way. In just the same manner, your answers to the above questions will help you understand how your body has been programmed. We tend to be quite hard on ourselves; so don't feel discouraged if you aren't feeling great about yourself yet, your answers might not all be positive. You're simply arming yourself with more information to help you shift.

Whether your thoughts and feelings are running in the background unconsciously or they are open and apparent, they will continue to remain the same until you actively do something to change them. These mental and emotional programs are what keep you stuck and prevent you from reaching your goals. Healthy change comes from encouragement on every level. This is why you need to be your biggest ally and think positively about yourself. Encouragement is a forward-moving, positive energy that supports your success. It is absolutely necessary for reaching your true potential.

Self-awareness and self-discovery come from being present. We are often unaware of our programming. This is true for both men and women. Moreover, these programs influence our behavior tremendously. Being present reveals what is keeping us from being powerful, and what we need to change. This is similar to discovering a computer virus. When you remove a computer virus, your computer is a powerful tool. However *with* a virus, your computer doesn't function well, and sometimes not at all. The virus is your negative programming. Discover it and you can remove it. Once removed, you'll be amazed by your results.

Understanding ourselves allows changes to occur at a deep level. Making changes on the inside builds a powerful foundation for a healthy lifestyle. Without this foundation, it is difficult to maintain healthy changes because the old issues, beliefs, and challenges that plague us, remain embedded in our psyches, and continue to interfere with our choices. This is why it is fundamental that we do some deep searching. Here are some questions that will further help your progress:

Your Questions to Yourself
When I think of who I am, how I am seen, and how I operate...
At this moment I feel...
At this moment I think...
At this moment I see...

Reframing your thinking is a necessary tool for transformation. Look back at your answers from your Self-Talk exercise. Take any statement you perceive as a negative comment, label, or thought and record it in your journal. Now turn this into a positive statement in larger, bolder print. You want to send a message to your brain that your positive statement is the correct one. If you have more than one negative statement, repeat the above process. When you catch yourself having these negative thoughts throughout the day, quickly reframe them into positive thoughts and repeat them to yourself.

Now take your positive statements and write them out 20 times each. If it feels good, write them out 20 more times. If you feel you need to tweak them, do so and then write the improved version 20 times. You are training your brain to think positively about yourself!

Tune into how you feel when you are writing out your positive statements. You'll know if you're on the right track if this process seems to flow and you feel good about your statements. If you find yourself resistant, keep practicing by writing these statements out daily. Your reframed statements will become positive affirmations.

> **"Cancel"** or **"Delete"** that which you don't want!

Cancel or Delete

If you hear or experience negative statements, thoughts, or influences that don't match up with your reframed, positive statements, immediately say the words "cancel" or "delete." This is a psychological remedy for addressing negative programming that has kept you down. When you use this technique often enough, you will train your brain to let go of old programming and embrace your new affirmations.

If you have never practiced this technique, it is easy to think that this is a silly word exercise. The reality is, these commands stop the negative domino effect in your mind. They will free you from the areas you have been stuck. Saying "cancel" or "delete" out loud also trains the people around you to stay positive. The more positive your environment is, the higher your chances are for succeeding.

It is also important to recognize the people, environments, and situations that continue to pollute you with negative thoughts and feelings. This will help you to change old patterns and value the people and environments that support you and your goals. Making sure that you maintain a supportive environment is imperative for your overall success.

Identify and Understand Your Hurdles

As you are gathering more knowledge about yourself, make sure to notice what is going on inside your mind and your body. Are you making progress? Are there areas that remain difficult to overcome, and if so, what seems to be the obstacle(s)? Understanding your inner makings is paramount to your success.

Recognizing Judgment

The key to becoming aware of your programming is to look for signs of judgment. Whether something is overtly said or covertly implied, it is judgment that is the main cause of our programming. When you become aware that you are comparing yourself to others, you'll often notice a pattern of judgment toward yourself. This has become pervasive in our high tech world where we are bombarded with images of people who have been air brushed, photo-shopped, and have endured endless plastic surgery. These images taunt our brains and we find ourselves asking, "Do I look like that?" "Can I ever look like that?"

Unrealistic Standards

In the late 1980's I observed a television series being filmed, in which the extras were referred to as "Perfect 10s." These extras happened to be beautiful women. Their role was to walk through scenes, lounge by pools in bathing suits, and sit in sexy outfits. They were part of the background of the show. When the director would call for four "10s" for the next scene, they would run to make up where their already amazing bodies became contoured and shaded to look even more defined. The result looked somewhat comical in real life but in the shots they would magically appear as the standard for beauty and body perfection. What did this do to the viewers who were judging themselves against an absurd and unreal measurement.

It's important to acknowledge that the media's standard of beauty doesn't truly exist in real life. It is created with make up, lighting, airbrushing, camera angles/lenses, and technology. This wreaks havoc on our self-esteem and has created a proliferation of photo-shopped images on social media websites. We now have contour makeup for everyday use, and have normalized plastic surgery. Whether we want to or not, we wind up comparing ourselves to the millions of images available on the Internet and television. When we take on the belief that the "doctored, retouched version of ourselves is the only way we can look, it is impossible to accept ourselves for who we really are.

Unachievable Results

Read the cover of any fitness magazine and you will see... "Look Younger in Just 5 Minutes!" "Insane Arms in 4 Easy Moves!" "Your 21-Day Total Body Makeover!" "Bikini Body in 7 Days!" These are all actual tag lines that I took from the covers of recent magazines. Our insatiable appetite for quick fixes and magical pills sell magazines filled with false promises.

What happens when we believe these false promises that sound too good to be true? We buy these magazines with high hopes. We follow these programs and, of course, we don't end up looking younger in 5 minutes, we don't have insane arms in four moves, we don't get a total body makeover in 21 days, or that bikini body in seven days. We then feel disappointed and depressed, and ultimately like a failure! This certainly is not positive reinforcement! Moreover, it produces a cycle of learned helplessness. The impact of unobtainable results and unreachable beauty standards has created an epidemic of low self-esteem and poor body image.

My History

I was diagnosed with scoliosis at a young age and it proved to provide me with many challenges. When I was 14, I pestered one of the football coaches to allow me to take his weightlifting class to learn to lift weights properly. He eventually trained me and this was tricky business and the experience gave me the understanding of what I now refer to as "Good Body Position."

Basically, Good Body Position is the precursor to all exercise and movement. There are specific body postures in ballet and yoga. There are alignment instructions for Pilates, Piyo, Resistance, and other exercise classes. I developed my philosophy for Good Body Position in the process of learning which muscles to develop first in order to build a continuously stronger body. I had to master proper body movements for each exercise in order to avoid back pain. Maintaining good body position all day was a requirement of my back, and so it became part of my life. Now I regularly teach this to my clients.

After years of working out in gyms, I began to notice that my frustration was increasing while I observed people working with their trainers. It was hard for me to watch people putting in time and effort to do exercises improperly. I was constantly aware of how poor body position was hindering a person's workout. In spite of their best efforts, they were not reaching their workout goals. I saw how discouraged they would become and how this worked to defeat them.

I tend to be on a mission to help people and it became more and more difficult for me to be in the gym without saying anything. I would spot someone out of the corner of my eye doing an exercise in one of two ways. They would either be just shy of injuring themselves or they would be doing an exercise in a completely useless manner due to poor form. I was constantly trying to figure out a way to help them. And so I started to jump in with many approaches…

"Excuse me, the way you are doing that exercise may create problems for you later on. Can I show you a way to do it differently?" (I always felt an urgency to intervene before they got hurt.)

"Hi, I'm Nina, I see you working so hard, can I show you a way to do that so you will get even better results?"

"Hi, would you be open to learning a way to do that exercise in a different way that could make it even more effective?"

My drive to help people to improve their health, led me to become a private trainer. Eventually my clients grew to the point where I needed to hire other trainers to work for me. I began a full health consulting business that did physical assessments, nutritional counseling, enzyme therapy, life coaching, and public speaking in the years that followed. My passion for good body position changed my life path. I then used it to improve my client's health. The results were that they got in great shape, experienced less body pain, and had fewer repetitive movement injuries.

Find a New Direction: Good Body Position Technique

Stand Straight

Stand as straight as possible and think of your head being lifted by a string. Think of the old skeleton in your science classroom that hung in perfect alignment from a chord.

Chin Tucked - Long Neck

Lengthen your neck and it will naturally bring your chin inward. This will keep you from placing your head in front of your neck and shoulders (pitched forward). Your head should be balanced on top of your spine. If it is in front of your spine, it forces the muscles in your neck to work harder and shifts your bone structure out of alignment.

Chest Up

Feel as though your body is lengthening toward the sky. As you raise your chest you will feel your stomach muscles lengthen and your belly move inward.

Squeeze "Angle Wings"

Visualize having giant wings like an angel. Squeeze the muscles together at the point of your mid-back where your shoulder blades are. This is the point your wings would attach to your body and will raise your chest further.

Stomach

Pull your abdominal muscles toward your spine.

Soft Knees

Make sure you don't lock your knees. Keep a slight bend. This will keep your leg muscles engaged and will help you burn more calories. Legs function like shock absorbers in this position.

Maintaining the above form gives you proper body position. It will also improve your metabolic rate, and cause less stress to your joints. Your circulation will also improve and you will feel more energized. In addition, you will have fewer injuries and your muscles will work more efficiently together. Your abs, leg muscles, chest, and back will all get a workout because you are engaging all of them now. This gives you better utilization of your muscles in general.

Your Weekly Commitment

My Activity

Get in Good Body Position:
- Start learning to train your body by slowing down your movements to ensure that you have good body position (i.e., during exercise, walking, running, etc.).
- Give yourself the time to learn this new skill by moving slowly and consciously.
- Create external reminders until you have incorporated your new posture into your life.
- Practice makes perfect body position. Keep practicing!

Put your "slow exercise" activities in your calendar. Train your body by slowing down your movements to achieve good body position (i.e., drop your treadmill speed to 2.5. Increase when you feel all of your muscles engaged).

- What do you notice?
- Is it difficult for you?
- Do you feel your muscles working?
- Do you feel your muscles working differently?

> **Your Accountability:** Share with your accountability partner your past and current mindset. Also share what you have learned about yourself, and what solutions you are implementing. Reframe your past, negative statements. Write down at least three new affirmations that have come from being present.

My Journal

Document how you feel. Make observations as you continue to incorporate your new practices into your life.

How is your body feeling while you are working on changing your posture?
(Your BSE)

- Scan your body from head to toe to see how you are doing. Make adjustments to keep yourself in good body position, moving properly. Do this consciously.

Make sure to include what you are thinking.
(Your MSE)

- Listen to your inner dialogue and feelings to see the connection that your mind has to your posture. Changing your posture can actually impact your thoughts in a positive way. A powerful posture provides self-confidence while a constricted posture lowers self-esteem. Again, this is a tool for self-awareness that will help you move forward.

Review your goals and distractions. Share any observations with your accountability partner and/or your journal.

Create reminders in your daily calendar, on your phone, and with sticky notes to do your BSE and MSE.

Your Thoughts and Notes:

Lost to Found in 90 Days: Chapter 7

Chapter 8:
Your Journal

Rachel's Journey

What do you do when you're passed overwhelmed and you're barely hanging in there? Maybe your job is stressing you out or you didn't get that promotion. Maybe you forgot to pay that bill and you wound up with a nasty late fee. More than likely it's a perfect storm of factors hitting you simultaneously. You may have a ton of unaddressed needs competing for your attention and you don't think you can add another ounce to your plate. Everyone has a limit.

Eventually, the point arrives when you're sick and tired of being sick and tired. You've tried a brisk walk, a hot bath, and calling your best friend. You've had that glass of wine and not even the bottle will help! You are a pot on the verge of boiling over. This was me at the end of November, right before I started my 90 day commitment. On the outside, I had a picture-perfect, "Facebook life." Everything appeared bright and shiny. With my uncanny ability to keep smiling no matter what, I had even fooled my nearest and dearest but I wasn't fooling myself.

Perception vs. Reality

My reality, however, was that I was feeling pretty low. And the funny thing is, I didn't even feel like I had the right to feel badly. I had a lot of positive things going on for me (career, friends, family, and a beautiful home). How on earth could I not be happy? I felt guilty and mystified. My core was telling me I wasn't fulfilled but what was missing exactly?

I had always heard about journaling. I was told it was a great way to vent – to get the thoughts swimming around your head, out on paper. I thought maybe I'd gain some clarity and peace of mind by allowing myself to "let go." I had actually tried journaling a long time ago. I remember my "Dear Diary" openers and wondered if this might unlock the mystery as to why I was struggling. I decided to give journaling another try and went to Target to find a new journal that felt good. I remember picking up several and turning them over in my hands. They just didn't feel right and I put them back down. I kept looking but nothing quite fit. And then I saw it: a lonely, little grey journal. On the cover was printed, "Life is what you make it to be." There was one left and it was perfect.

I Bet She Journals

I made a promise to myself that I would journal every day for 90 days. This was going to be my new thing. I was committed to seeing where it would lead. I envisioned myself as one of those people you read about and think, "Oh she is so centered and connected. I bet she journals."

When you first start journaling it may feel a bit awkward. My first day's attempt was quite colorful. I eagerly grabbed my new pen. I'm left handed and specifically got one with fast-drying ink (fellow left handers know what I'm talking about!). I poured a glass of Pellegrino (in a wine glass!), picked a seat at my dining room table, opened my new journal, and sat down to write. What proceeded was not what I had planned. I stared at that page for about an hour. I had no idea what to write about. I thought this process would just naturally FLOW. Instead, I found myself completely bottled up.

Undeterred, I told myself to find another journal-writing location I chose my bedroom. I grabbed my journal and pen but forgot my Pellegrino. This could take a while! Finally in my comfy bed with everything I needed, I found myself staring at its cover. I opened it, took a deep breath… AND… nothing! Nothing?! Come on Rachel! This is your moment!! Be *that* girl!! This was not going according to plan.

Journals and Blankets

I walked back out to the living room and conceded. I landed in the nook of my couch – my go-to snuggle spot. I grabbed my favorite blanket (I'm obsessed with snuggly blankets), and turned on the TV. Yep, instead of journaling, I flipped over to Lifetime. Very productive indeed. I started to watch a movie. You know, the one about a mother's brother killing his sister, who was really her father in disguise. Yes, I'm being facetious! I proceeded to half-watch the movie. In this relaxed state, I began to let my mind wander.

Every single day when I came home from work, I threw on my favorite yoga pants, a comfy tank top, and I'd sit in that very same spot under a blanket. This was my consummate unwinding ritual. I realized this was my happy place. The place I felt most at ease. And that was it for me. I grabbed my remote, turned off the TV, and ran to my room for my journal.

Something just clicked. The words began to FLOW! All of my pent up energy, feelings, emotions, doubts, and fears came tumbling out. I was amazed by how fast my pen was moving. I didn't even know if I was making sense but it didn't matter. This was just for me. I was finally letting it all out. No one would read this stuff. No one would judge me. And this is how my journal became my "non-judgmental best friend."

My journal aka
"my non-judgmental best friend"

And so it began. Every day, at least once a day, I would sit in my magic comfy-spot and journal my heart out. It felt GOOD!! Now, I'll admit, I didn't hit all 90 days but I journaled most of them. This process was amazingly powerful. Documenting my 90 days brought me to a heightened sense of self awareness that worked wonders in my life. When I reviewed my journal at the end of my journey, I could literally see myself evolving, growing, and changing as a person.

Quiet Time

The new me left work to go to the gym (if I hadn't gone that morning), ate a healthy dinner at home, got in comfy clothes, made a cup of tea, and journaled in my sacred space. *Skipping* happy hours, wine, appetizer and dessert calories, and zone-out time in front of reality TV made an immense improvement in my life. It was thoroughly transformative.

I started craving my quiet time and, in the process, I gained the clarity I had been searching for. During my 90 days, I thought I was "just" journaling. What I didn't realize was that I was actually setting new standards for myself. I was teaching myself how to care for myself and be treated by others. I was examining all of the experiences I had not fully let myself internalize. It was there on the couch that I finally granted myself the grace for getting a divorce. I had been holding onto guilt for the past two years and it wasn't allowing me to move forward. The ongoing conversation with myself through journaling allowed me to work through the guilt and come to this conclusion.

My biggest joy in life is making people happy, so the thought of hurting anyone is horrendous to me. To forgive myself for any hurt I may have caused my ex was a huge deal. Journaling helped me finally come to terms with the fact that I had tried everything in my power to make my marriage work. I left with my side of the table clean. Acknowledging this to myself helped me truly move on.

Your Story Is Just Beginning

Throughout my journaling, I found kindness and grace for myself and others. Releasing the painful feelings I had held onto for so long was beyond liberating. I didn't realize I had been holding onto my ex with such negative emotions. I discovered a deeper level of compassion for both of us and truly sent him off with prayers and best wishes that I genuinely meant. I let go of the shame I felt over getting divorced. It was now just part of my past. And my future was just beginning!

My nonjudgmental best friend now travels with me. If I have a moment and need to vent or share something exciting – to my journal I head! It's a potent and freeing process that continues to lead to self-discovery.

Rachel's Journaling Tips
Pick a journal that feels good to you. The right one will stand out from the crowd.
Create a ritual around your journaling time. Make this a special thing you look forward to. You can light a candle, turn on calming music (think yoga/massage), and find your happy, sacred space to cozy-up with a blanket.

Rachel's Journaling Tips

Keep your journaling time free of distractions (away from your cell phone, TV, Facebook).

Stay consistent and journal daily. This is how the discoveries and breakthroughs come.

Keep your journal by your bed, in case you wake in the middle of the night and need to do a "mind dump" to release any anxiety or confusion... or to record your brilliant revelations!

Nina's Knowledge: Knowledge Is Power

Stay in Curiosity

How will journaling help you lose weight and get in better shape? The components of getting healthy are simple but making changes can still be challenging. Understanding your life, your environment, your thoughts, your wants, your needs, your obstacles, your patterns, your habits, etc., provides you with immense knowledge about yourself. Knowledge is power! The wisdom in those three simple words is beyond measure.

Journaling is your tool to gather the knowledge that will transform your life. It is t he most effective means for catching the thoughts that run through your mind, and recognizing the patterns and trends that govern your life. Journaling identifies your obstacles clearly, and helps you find solutions to overcome them. In essence, journaling provides you with a much deeper understanding of yourself! It is this understanding that becomes the motivation to transform your life.

Knowledge Isn't Good or Bad

Knowledge isn't good or bad – it just is! Stay in a state of curiosity. Curiosity has a catalytic energy. Without it you won't access the knowledge that provides you with a deeper understanding of yourself. Staying in curiosity removes your judgment and allows you to analyze the information you discover about yourself. It provides you with the ability to be open to all of the information you glean, and remain in a neutral place.

Developing a neutral perspective about your self-discoveries is necessary to fully accept and process the multitude of experiences that have brought you to this point in time. Once you can see why you are where you are, self-compassion and self-forgiveness naturally follow.

Staying in curiosity may sound detached or removed. It is common for this to bother people initially because it is so foreign. However, you are simply giving yourself the opportunity to observe your life as a neutral witness. This will not stop you from being a caring person. It will, however, allow you to have breakthroughs. Let's work through a scenario to see what staying in curiosity looks like.

Knowledge in Action

I had a client who had a binge-eating event one evening. When reviewing the situation, we came to discover that her trigger was a conversation with her mother. By remaining in curiosity, she was able to see the event without the onslaught of negative emotions that normally accompany self-criticism. Remember, we're giving up the habit of judging ourselves.

My client realized that having conversations with her mother challenged her. She also realized she could choose to manage her relationship differently. This breakthrough gave her the ability to forgive herself. She now had insight into a pattern that had been holding her back. With this new knowledge, she was able to overcome a longstanding challenge. Here's how she processed the event:

Nina: "What happened last night?"

Client: "I ate a bunch of ice cream and potato chips. I seem to do this after I talk with my mother. My mother drives me crazy sometimes."

Nina: "Describe the whole evening."

Client: "I came home and was doing laundry and cleaning the bathrooms. Then she called."

Nina: "How do you feel about what you were doing?"

Client: "I hate cleaning the bathrooms but I love when they are done. So I push through the chores in order to get to the end quickly."

Nina: "Was there anything you felt like you were missing in order to clean?"

Client: "Yep. I had friends coming by the next day so I skipped my cardio in lieu of cleaning the bathrooms. I felt like I had no choice."

Nina: "What happened before you got home?"

Client: "I was working. Actually, I had a tough day at work. Nothing seemed to go smoothly."

Nina: "How did that make you feel?"

Client: "I generally feel under pressure at work but that day was especially intense."

Nina: "What were you doing when your mom called?"

Client: "I was in the middle of scrubbing my tub. I had to drop everything, fumble around, and try to get to my phone with wet hands."

Nina: "What was your mom calling about?"

Client: "She wanted to talk about my sister's birthday next month."

Nina: "How did that make you feel?"

Client: "Crazy. It is a month away. I don't have the luxury of thinking about next week, much less something a month away."

Nina: "So what happened on the phone?"

Client: "I tried to get off the phone but had to listen to her go into every little detail about party planning. Meanwhile I was trying to keep my hands from dripping all over the floor."

Nina: "Did you tell her how you were feeling or that you needed to go?"

Client: "No, I can't be that way with my mom."

Nina: "What happened after the call?"

Client: "I had to clean up the new mess I created by answering the phone! Then I finished cleaning the tub, and continued to do my laundry for the next couple of hours."

Nina: "When did you start eating?"

Client: "It was quite late. I didn't have time to make dinner so I started grabbing anything. I really wanted ice cream."

This is an example of how staying in curiosity can lead you to vital information about yourself. The idea is to dig deeper and deeper to find the root cause for your behavior and feelings. The more questions you ask yourself, the more information you uncover. Most people will find that there is more than one reason for a particular pattern to show up in their life. In order to clear harmful patterns, we need to know their origins. Staying in curiosity is the key to a secret door. When you open this door, you will discover many things about yourself that can help you move forward.

Find a New Direction: Journal to a Healthy Life

Journaling gives you the opportunity to deeply understand what's actually happening inside your mind and body. If you can stay in curiosity, you will find that it is easier to address your challenges and the rough cycles in your life when you find yourself spiraling. Use your journal to continue to question yourself. The information you gather can be a powerful motivating force in your life. This is also an incredibly effective way to find creative solutions to your challenges.

Journaling is much like cleaning out your closet. Once you pull everything out, you can pick and choose what you want to keep and what you want to discard. The process of journaling enables you to determine where change can be most effective in your life.

Ask yourself the following questions:

- What do I need?
- What do I have?
- What isn't working?
- What do I need to eliminate that no longer serves me?

Journaling is an opportunity to look at what we are holding onto and determine whether or not to let go of it.

Journaling doesn't have to be hard. Start slow. Block out 10 minutes a day to journal. You don't have to commit to any topic, just journal consistently. You can choose a blank journal or one that poses a different question on each page. If you prefer, you can journal on your smartphone or computer There's something out there for everyone. It doesn't matter what you choose, just start.

> There is an amazing daily journaling
> feature in your **L2F90 App!**

If you find yourself having difficulty with this process, just record yourself talking. Talk about whatever is in your head. There is no judgment.

I had a client with insomnia a while back. He was a successful businessman with a high-pressure position. I asked him to journal for two minutes right before bed and immediately after he woke up. In one week's time he made quite the discovery regarding his chronic condition. He realized that he was holding onto the belief that sleep wasn't as important as work. He felt that he didn't have the time to sleep and, therefore, shouldn't. Through journaling he found the reason why he couldn't sleep… he wasn't allowing himself to! This was entirely unconscious on his part. Regardless of how many conversations I had with him on the importance of sleep, he was unable to allow himself to do so until he had his "Aha" moment.

Self-Compassion

Journaling can bring us to a new level of self-compassion. This actually works to raise our self-esteem. Being able to read through our entries gives us pause to allow compassion for everything we've endured. Journaling helps us to see ourselves. We realize how hard we've worked. We process what we've lost. We become aware of how we've hurt, etc.

Most of the time, we don't process these experiences fully. Our lives get so busy that we skip over compassion for ourselves and save it for our loved ones. Adding ourselves to our list of loved ones is fundamental for self-compassion. Journaling allows us to be truly present and honest about our journey and find a level of self-acceptance that is powerfully healing. Our compassion for ourselves, coupled with our bolstered self-esteem, converts into life-force energy that helps us to move in a positive direction.

Weekly Commitment

Your Activity

Your journal is your resource to document your experiences, feelings, observations, and "Aha" moments. View a recent entry of yours from a place of curiosity.

- What event did you choose to examine?
- How did you experience this event when you looked at it from a detached point of view?
- Has this changed your perception of the experience?
- Would you like to (or do you need to) change anything regarding this?

Schedule your journal time and set up a weekly review time.

> **Your Accountability:** Share your experience with your L2F90 accountability partner and get his/her feedback. Ask each other what observations you've made regarding your experiences.

Your Journal

Write 10 minutes a day in your journal. Add another 5 minutes in your schedule to review past entries.

- BSE – Body Status Exam – Check in with how your body is feeling.
- MSE – Mental Status Exam – Check in with what you are thinking.

Review your goals:

- What did you do differently this week?
- How has this made you feel differently?
- Examine your fitness routine. How are you doing with it?
- What are your new successes/accomplishments?
- How did you show compassion to yourself this week?
- What activity added to your self-esteem this week?

Sign a weekly commitment to your goals that keeps you accountable.

Your Thoughts and Notes:

Lost to found in 90 Days: Chapter 8

Chapter 9:
Your Relationship Standards and Allies

Rachel's Journey

I found that my transformative journey contained several key elements that significantly moved me forward. I've shared that I felt stuck for a long time and getting unstuck was incredibly empowering. In order to move forward, we often have to face some personal "hot spots." My "hot spot" was about to come into full view and I was admittedly nervous about sharing it.

Comfortable Vulnerability

For me, this may be the most important chapter of the entire book. Sharing my process was quite the challenge because it made made me feel very vulnerable. While vulnerability is not a comfortable place for anyone to reside, it probably won't come as a surprise to you that I preferred having full authority and control over the outcomes in my life! I was entering into uncharted waters but I knew I couldn't share this program if I wasn't 100% authentic.

I discussed in the previous chapter how journaling about my divorce was therapeutic for me. However, the reason this chapter was so hard for me to write was because I worried my honesty would hurt my ex-husband. This was a paralyzing thought for me. My rule had been to never publicly talk about our divorce, and there are many people I deal with who don't even know I was married. So after making every excuse under the sun to avoid this chapter, I finally realized that I had been holding the misconception that I had control over my ex's feelings. When I acknowledged that I only have control over my own feelings and reactions, I allowed myself to open up about the one area I had consistently kept locked down.

By now you know that I am professionally driven. This is the area I'm most confident. I regularly write out my business goals and share them with my team. My partner and I have a vision statement for our business and we adhere to it. We know exactly how many deals we need to close to hit our annual goals, and we know the standards we demand of ourselves professionally.

Personal Standards

I knew my professional standards inside and out… but what about my personal life? Shouldn't I have standards for that too? As I looked back at my marriage, I realized I never truly had clarity on what I wanted out of a partner. I was raised with two parents who have been married 37 years, and my dad still calls my mom his bride. They hold hands at the grocery store and leave little love notes around the house for each other. I grew up being called a "princess" by my dad. They made it look easy! As a result, I really thought marriage would be a breeze.

I remember thinking that I would meet a great guy, fall in love, and live "happily ever after." So easy, right? It's important to share that I love marriage in general, loved being a wife, and really looked forward to being a mother (still do!). I met my ex-husband when I was 24 years old. He was fun, good looking, and fresh out of the Marine Corps. At that age, I didn't know what I wanted or who I was. About the only thing we knew for certain was that we both wanted to have a kid someday, and that we looked really great in photos (it's the important things, right?).

In the beginning of our relationship, we got along great and laughed a lot. It seemed natural that we should get married. At that age, I didn't know to ask the BIG questions that really matter: What do you want out of life? How do you communicate love? What matters most to you? What do you want your legacy to be? I knew we had lots of differences in our upbringing and they shaped our views on life but I thought if you loved someone enough, you could get through anything.

The Truth

The truth was, our differences made us incompatible as partners and overtime these differences became more pronounced and challenging to deal with. To sum it up, we went through one good year, and four very hard ones. We were two, very different people who wanted different things out of life. We had no similar interests to bond over and our ambition didn't match up. I just didn't know back then how important these factors were for having a good marriage.

I stayed in that marriage about two years longer than I should have because I didn't want to have any regrets. I went to marriage counseling and life coaching, but ultimately we were just too different. He wasn't happy. I wasn't happy. We no longer talked. We stopped doing things together and we became more like roommates than husband and wife.

I realized I wanted more for myself. We both deserved more. Filing for separation was hard. Filing for divorce was even harder. In spite of this, it also felt right. When I left my marriage, I remember feeling relieved, but also feeling horrible about feeling such relief. For the first time in years, I could breathe. I felt like a huge weight had been lifted. Instead of feeling sad, I felt light... and I needed lightness.

I threw myself into a 13-week divorce recovery group. I was still wrestling with the guilt and shame I felt over getting a divorce but having put in the sincere effort to work on our marriage, I knew there was no other way for us. I was determined to improve myself and I wanted to make sure that my next relationship would be healthy, loving, and deeply compatible.

My Worth

The big shift happened when I realized what I was worth. With this realization came the epiphany that I deserved to be happy. I deserved to be with someone who wanted the same things out of life. I wanted a healthy relationship with an equal partner who has similar interests. I didn't want to stay in a marriage because of guilt and fear over becoming another "divorce statistic."

The big shift happened when I realized what I was worth.

It's now two years later and we've both moved on. I even saw a picture of him recently and thought he looked great! He looked happy. He looked light. It made me smile. He deserves happiness just as much as I do. Journaling over my 90 days had me come around full circle. My ex wasn't a bad guy. He was actually a really good guy. He just wasn't the right guy for me... and I wasn't the right girl for him.

I realized that as difficult as the divorce was, I wouldn't change anything. I heard a great quote that people come into your life for a reason, a season or a lifetime. For me, my ex husband came into my life to teach me some important lessons about relationships. In the process of going through our marriage and divorce, I found my inner strength, and ultimately I learned a tremendous amount about self-worth and personal standards. While I can't speak for him, I am grateful for the experience. It wasn't easy but I don't regret it. It's just part of my journey.

My Personal Vision Statement

It's important to reiterate how fundamental it was for me to be journaling during my 90 days. I was amazed by the new level of clarity that was showing up in my life. I think It was about day 45 when I thought about what dating would be like for me once I'd completed my 90 day challenge. Would I go back on dating sites? Where would I meet guys? And then it hit me... I was no longer focusing on the external factors like what my perfect guy would look like. I was thinking about what he would be like. What did he think about? What truly mattered to him? What did he want in life? How was he brought up? What were his interests?

The next thing that happened was probably my favorite part of this entire grand experiment. I got out my trusty journal and decided to draft a personal vision statement – in the same way I had already done so for my business. This would be my declaration for what my perfect mate would be like. I would get clarity on who he was, and what I wanted out of a partner. With my self worth intact, I realized I really was a treasure, and that it would take a pretty amazing guy to snatch me up!

So this is what I did. I wrote out the words: Affection, Drive, Family, Faith, Communication, Intimacy, Community, Food, Pastimes, Support, Chivalry and Courting, Health, Financial, Humor, and Looks. It was funny, I remember when I first made my list, I didn't even have "Looks" on it. A friend of mine mentioned this to me, and that's how I knew things had really changed. My emphasis had turned to who my other half would be, not what they would look like. I am human, however, and being attracted to my partner does matter, so I added "Looks" to my list. Here's an example of my journal entries to help you get started.

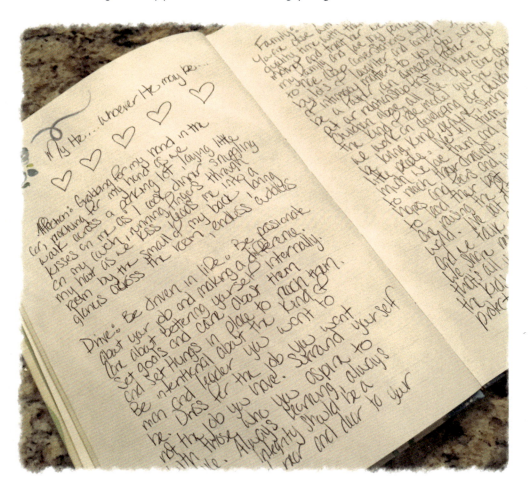

The Value of Clarity

This exercise proved really helpful for me. I was creating a standard for myself that had previously been missing. I made sure to include all of the important things that mattered to me in a relationship. Without this clarity, I might have repeated the same lesson I had already been through with my first marriage. Thank God I now knew what was truly important to me in a relationship.

Another significant discovery came when I realized what I wouldn't do without. No one is perfect, and finding a guy with every quality on my list might have been rare but there were some things on my list that were non-negotiables. Faith, communication, and health were at the top of my list. It was a really powerful thing to discover. From that point on I knew that when I chose to get into a relationship with someone, I would take my time, really get to know them, and see how they matched up with my new vision statement. I deserved someone amazing!

An even cooler part to all of this was that I started to have standards for all of my relationships, including my friends, business colleagues, and family members. I realized that if you have high standards for yourself in relationships, you begin to want to raise your standards with other things as well. I was creating a great life a nd now I had this new clarity on how to get there! I was 45 days in, and I felt like a new woman!

Realizing that I had control over who I shared my life with, had an enormous impact on me. I knew life would never be the same. As quoted by one of my great mentors, Jim Rohn, "You are the average of the 5 people you spend the most time with." So the question becomes who do you choose to surround yourself with? If they are not headed in the same direction the new-you is heading in, then you may have some difficult decisions to make. Don't be afraid to edit your peer group!

You are the average of the five people you spend the most time with.

Now it's your turn. Make a personal vision statement for what you want and need in life. Get clear on your non-negotiables. What are the most important aspects you require in your primary relationship?

My Tinder Heart

When I stopped dating for 90 days, I wasn't sure how this would affect my life. It was, however, nice to take a break from getting ready twice a day (i.e., putting on a new outfit after work and freshening up my hair and makeup). When I deleted the dating apps from my phone, I felt an immediate sense of relief. There was no more stopping mid-email to "swipe right". I didn't realize how much those little notification dings distracted me!

A funny thing happened when I eliminated dating, my productivity at the office went way up! I was focused, driven, and ready to take on new goals that had previously intimidated me. I remember on day 17, we had 9 new escrow accounts and my business partner Matt said, "Ummm, Rach, you are never dating again!" It was freeing not being tied to those apps and being able to focus on my goals.

I now noticed that when I went to the grocery store, I was no longer scoping out men in the aisles. I focused on my grocery list and got out of there faster. When I went out with my girlfriends, I wasn't looking across the table or scanning the room to see who was around me. I was present with those around me. Imagine that. I was paying full attention to the people I was with. I even took it one step further. I put my cell phone away whenever I was out with my friends. I no longer cared if I got a message from a guy or not. I was committed to making the most of my time with my friends and treating them with the respect they deserved.

I realized people deserved my full attention. Everyone is busy, and if I made plans to spend time with someone, I was going to be fully present in my conversations with them. This was something I had to think about at first but as I did it on a regular basis, it became a new habit.

To change your life, change your habits.

When I became fully present with the people I spent time with, the quality of my friendships began to deepen. I was allowing myself to have uninterrupted, bonding time with longtime friends. What a gift! My relationships with those who mattered got stronger. I was really liking this.

Nina's Knowledge: Relationships Standards and Allies

Valuable Connections

"Relationship" is defined as the way in which two or more concepts, objects, or people are connected. Do you pay attention to who you are in a relationship with? In working with clients who you choose to surround yourself with is never more apparent than when looking at individual outcomes. People who become successful with their health are much more likely to have the people around them who also care about their health and are contributing to their success. Conversely, people who struggle with their health often don't feel great about themselves and are surrounded by others who feel the same way and contribute to their struggles. This was never more obvious than with one of my clients.

I had a severely obese client who was unable to walk or move around. Before our first meeting, I was told that she had problems with her hip. I went to her home, rang the bell, and someone other than my client answered the door. I walked in to meet my new client and found her lounging in a recliner. I introduced myself and asked, "What would you like me to help you with?" She laughed and said, "I am fat and I can't walk. I spend most of my day sitting right here in this chair."

After asking more details about her injury, I asked how she was currently getting around and how she got food. She said that she used special crutches, but mostly that she didn't move. She said that her housekeeper and husband brought food to her. The more I learned about her, the more it became apparent that she really loved to eat.

There were things she loved to eat and she said she absolutely couldn't stop eating them if they were available. I said, "Well, if you can't get around except using crutches, that could keep you from having those foods in the house or even going into the kitchen. If we got rid of the food in the house that didn't support your weight loss, the only option would be to eat healthy." She said, "That doesn't help because those foods are always in the house and someone can bring them to me."

Supporters and Saboteurs

It was unbelievable how true that last statement was for her and many other people in similar situations. Even though my client's husband was the person that asked me to help his wife, he was the one sabotaging her goal of walking again. He had created a relationship with her that enabled her to be morbidly obese. He seemed to enjoy the power of controlling everything in the house, including her. (He would have the housekeeper bake her favorite unhealthy foods to have around even when she said she was committed to eating healthy. She would work at turning away foods offered to her and lose 10 lbs in a month, only to have her husband reward her with food from her favorite restaurant.

This example is so blatant that it seems easy to see, but it wasn't to the people in the situation. There may be relationships in your life that are less obviously detrimental but are still interfering with your positive changes.

To maintain this kind of dysfunctional connection we have to have become powerless somewhere within ourselves. You might think that someone has your best interest at heart, when in reality there is something within them that is struggling with you reaching your goals. There are many things that define the type of connection we have with others. These things will impact who we choose to have in our lives. When we feel shaky, we can look at ourselves and our relationships to discover why. If you find yourself not hitting your goals, it isn't just about you, it is also about who you are surrounding yourself with. We can end up amplifying our weakness if we are aren't surrounded by the right people. Knowing about you will assist you in addressing your deficits and help you make choices to grow and move away from your challenges rather than add to them.

Find a New Direction: Knowing Yourself and Others

Knowing Yourself

What are our internal issues that make us feel insecure, uncertain, small, conflicted, etc.? Who do you associate with these feelings?

Power Questions
Do you feel powerful?
Who makes you feel more powerful? Less??
What makes you feel powerful?

Security Questions
Do you feel secure?
Who makes you feel more secure? Less??
How do they make you feel secure?

Laughter Questions
Do you laugh?
Who makes you laugh?

Your relationship with yourself is the foundation of your powerful health. It is the key to your future. It identifies the path to your goals. It determines your relationships with others.

Take inventory of the people you are connected to.

Which friends, family members, business associates, or others can you list as answers to the following questions?

Knowing Others
Who knows your dreams?
Who supports your passions?
Who adores you?
Who admires you?
Who "gets" you?
Who do you laugh with?
Who do you like to do nothing with?
Who knows what you would enjoy doing in your free time?
Who do you share your opinions with?

Weekly Commitment

Your Activity

- Knowing Yourself
  - Journal about what you observe in your answers.
  - Are you surprised about anything?
  - Do you see any patterns?

- Knowing Others
  - List the people you spend time with throughout your day. Which people are listed in the "Knowing Others" list?
  - Note how often you spend time with or talk to the people on your "Knowing Others" list.

> **Your Accountability:** Connect with your accountability partner to discuss your observations.

Your Journal

Reread your answers in the exercise above and write in your journal for 10 minutes a day. Make your own list of the words that matter to you in a relationship, like Rachel did. What are your standards? Review past entries in your L2F90 Chronicles.

Review your goals in your journal:

- Note the connection of those around you to your successes, your goals, your changes, and anything that you have been doing differently.
- Sign a weekly commitment to your goals that keeps you accountable.
- BSE – Body Status Exam – Check in with how your body is feeling.
- MSE – Mental Status Exam – Check in with what you are thinking.

Your Thoughts and Notes:

Lost to Found in 90 Days: Chapter 9

Chapter 10:
Your Goals and Lists

Rachel's Journey

I have always envisioned a BIG life for myself. I want a highly successful career. I want to be a motivational speaker who travels throughout the US making a positive difference in people's lives. In addition, I want to be a famous author and singer. I also want a gorgeous custom-built home and two vacation homes. And finally, I want a perfect family with a ridiculously handsome husband and two gorgeous kids (boy and girl). I want to share my big life with an amazing group of friends who also achieve their dreams. And I want a close relationship with my parents who are fit and healthy. That's not too much to ask for, right?

I once read an article about goal setting in Forbes magazine that made a huge impression on my life and is well worth sharing:

> We hear a lot about the importance of goal setting but most of us don't have clear and measurable goals to work towards. Even fewer of us actually have those goals written down. Lewis Carroll says, "Any road will get you there, if you don't know where you are going," but how important are goals really and if they are vital, how can we make them most effective? There was a fascinating study conducted on the 1979 Harvard MBA program where graduate students were asked "Have you set clear, written goals for your future and made plans to accomplish them?" The result: only 3% had written goals and plans, 13% had goals but they weren't in writing, and 84% had no goals at all. Ten years later, the same group was interviewed again and the result was absolutely mind-blowing. The 13% of the class who had goals but did not write them down was earning twice the amount of the 84% who had no goals. **The 3% who had written goals were earning, on average, ten times as much as the other 97% of the class combined!**
>
> – Excerpt from *"Why You Should Be Writing Down Your Goals,"* by Ashley Feinstein. Posted to Forbes.com on April 8, 2014.

I have business goals, fitness goals, and overall health goals. I have goals for how many books I want to read each year and where I want to vacation each year. It is one thing to have goals and quite another to actually commit them to paper. The simple act of writing **and seeing your goals on paper increases the likelihood of you reaching them ten-fold.** Sharing them with the people in your life makes you more accountable to your goals and further increases your success rate.

I write out my goals and then form a plan for how I'm going to achieve them. In my experience, I have found that it works best to see the end goal, and work backwards to create the path to achieve them.

Take weight loss, for example. As I sit here writing this, I have 12 pounds to lose in order to reach my ideal weight. Here's my process:

Rachel's Process	
1. Write my goal	"Lose 12 Pounds"
I know my body, and if I consistently eat clean and work out, I can lose 1 pound per week. (1-2 pounds of weight loss per week is healthy and sustainable)	
2. Do the math and record it	"Lose 12 pounds in 12 weeks."

Rachel's Process	
3. Break it down to measurable weekly or daily goals	Break down the goal into the required steps. Include supporting data. "A pound is 3,500 calories. To lose one pound per week you need to eat 500 less calories per day (3,500 / 7 = 500). If your daily caloric burn is 1,800 calories then eating 1,300 per day will reduce your weight by 1 pound per week."
4. Do the things that will help me reach my goal	This sets my path for attaining what I set out to accomplish.

Here are some additional tips for success:

Tips for Success	
1. Get an accountability partner and share your goal.	This is someone to workout with daily. I am much more likely to get my butt out of bed if I have a friend meeting me at the gym. I won't stand her up. You get my drift!
2. Hang a "goal picture" on your fridge of how you'd like to look.	This can be a photo of me at my ideal weight or it can be a magazine image of a body I admire. As previously mentioned, I make sure the image is of someone with my same height and build. My goal must be reachable. I can lose weight but growing another foot is unrealistic!
3. Make sure that your environment supports your goals.	For weight loss, I go through my cabinets and clear out any junk food. If it's not in my kitchen, I'm less likely to eat it.
4. Pick two days a week to prepare healthy meals for the rest of the week.	I did this Sundays and Wednesdays.
5. Log your food and water intake.	I've found that if I write it down, my accountability partner can check it and I'm less likely to eat that piece of chocolate cake!
6. Include your workouts in your calendar.	Give these the same level of importance as a client appointment.

	Tips for Success	
7.	Track your progress.	Weigh in weekly at the same time and take measurements. I usually do this after I shower.
8.	Take "before and after" photos every 30 days to mark your progress.	It is empowering to see change!

Goals are beautiful things. They demand clarity. They demand action. They demand discipline. When reached, they command self-respect and satisfaction. They are your pathways for attaining your simplest desires all the way to your biggest dreams. Without them, life can be directionless. However, you must have a plan for attaining your goals because a goal without a plan is just a wish.

A goal without a plan is just a wish.

Remember, it's not who you are now, but who you are becoming. Live, breathe, sleep, and eat like the person you want to become. In time you'll realize you have become that person! Making goals will help you reach the highest and best version of yourself!

Lost   Found

Making a List

Let's move on to lists! I have always been a "list person." Listing my goals makes me happy, mostly because I like to be able to check things off my list! I get a real sense of satisfaction when I've accomplished a goal. Lists also help me manage the umpteen things swirling around my head. If I put these down on a list, I am more likely to get them done, and things don't slip through the cracks.

I used to only make lists for tasks I needed to complete in my immediate future. In my 90 day program, I added three more lists to my life. I now have a DREAM LIST, a JOY LIST, and a GRATITUDE LIST.

My DREAM LIST includes all of the things that I want for myself. It is a way for me to keep them in the foreground so that I am more likely to manifest them.

My JOY LIST includes all of the things that make me happy. Happiness is ultimately what we're all striving for and it actually makes me happy to think of these things and write them down! This list keeps me in touch with what I love to do, and makes me more likely to do them!

My most important list came in the form of my GRATITUDE LIST. In the quiet of my 90 day journey, I had nothing to distract me from thinking about my dreams and my ideal life. I realized just how much I had to be thankful for so I wrote it all down.

Thanksgiving Every Day of the Year

I started feeling so good writing this list that I added it to my morning journal time. I would write down three things I was grateful for every day and an amazing thing occurred. I found myself regularly scanning my day for the positives. Unknowingly, I had created the mental habit of looking for the good in my life, and every time I acknowledged it, I experienced a burst of happiness.

In the beginning, this list was easy. I found myself writing things like, "I'm thankful for my family and friends." As the days went on, I had to dig deeper and my list began to surprise and amaze me. I was grateful for my ability to forgive and to receive forgiveness. I was grateful for the ability to heal. I wrote things like, "I am thankful for my divorce and the lessons it taught me." "I am thankful for the grace God grants me to start fresh every day."

Trust me, if you wake up with a feeling of gratitude, the rest of your day goes so much better! I began to think of all that I had, rather than all that I didn't. The most important part was that I started to be thankful for ME. I accepted all of my quirks, challenging lessons, and my unique and beautiful heart. I embraced my imperfections and knew that I was imperfectly perfect just the way I was.

My gratitude list helped me forgive myself. I started to grant myself permission to be just as I was. It was OK that I got a divorce. It was OK that I missed the gym that morning. It was OK that I said "No" to hosting an event because I needed quiet time. I was valuing my time, my needs and ultimately my worth! I was owning the life I had in a whole new way and I was so grateful for it.

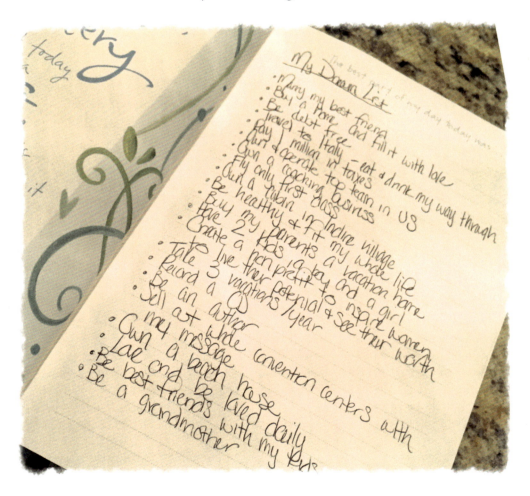

Nina's Knowledge: Powerful Lists

Martin Luther King's famous words, "I have a dream..." declared an immense vision for the future. In order to reach your mega-size dream or goal, you need a mega-size list! Knowing the destination you want to reach is the first part. The second part is finding the way.

To reach your goals you'll need a map. Your map is actually your list, which comprises the means and the method for attaining your goals. I wish I could share with you a magnificent quote about lists to inspire you. "I have a list..." doesn't exactly produce goose bumps but it makes the point. You need a well thought out list to reach your goals and ultimate dreams.

When you set your goals down on paper, you are telling the Universe you are committed to reaching them. Many people have goals they never reach, simply because they don't take them seriously and write them down..

A successful goal requires several steps. You'll need to map out how to get your desired effect. This will involve creating a list of steps to reach your goal. You'll need to be self-disciplined and make some sacrifices along the way. And you'll need to have faith in yourself to believe you can reach your goal.

Dreams, Gratitude, and Your Goals

Dreams

Daydreamers are often given a bad rap. If you've ever been told to get your head out of the clouds and stop daydreaming, let me be the one to tell you that your ability to dream is a gift! Great imaginations are responsible for the most creative solutions and remarkable designs on the planet. Olympic athletes have some of the best imaginations because they can see themselves breaking records and winning the gold medal.

Your dreams can serve you well, so don't give them up and don't stop dreaming. Even if you have a hard time figuring out how to accomplish your dreams, you're way ahead of the pack. You know where you want to go. While you can find others to help you reach your goals, no one except you can decide where you want to go! Since this program is your journey from Lost to Found, we'll walk you through the process for reaching your goals.

Gratitude

What does gratitude have to do with dreaming, goal setting, and making lists? If we aren't grateful for what we already have, it will be extremely hard to accomplish our dreams and goals. Focusing on what we don't have will only create more of the same. The Universe has a way of giving back to us what we put out there.

So if we focus on what we don't have, we'll continue to not have what we want. However, if we are grateful for all that we do have, the Universe will provide even more. So make sure to scan your horizon for all of the things you are grateful for in your life, and thank the Universe for taking such good care of you. Then thank the Universe for taking care of your dreams and goals!

Goals

Make sure that your goals align with the person you want to be. This is the person you are nurturing and becoming during your 90 days. Often people's old patterns have a way of sneaking up on them and competing against the direction they are moving.

Your self-discovery has given you information about yourself that can help guide you. Once you have removed the judgment, you can formulate your goals. Just make sure that what you want to accomplish serves the highest and best version of yourself. Then, create your list to get there.

Find Your New Direction: Create Your List to Reach Your Goal

One of the challenges I hear most commonly from my clients is that they have no problem envisioning what they want for themselves but they have no idea how to get it. So let's include some examples and walk you through the process.

1. **Start with a generalized health statement that you want to realize.**

    I am healthy and fit, so I am able to...
    I am healthy and fit, so I would like to...
    Being healthy and fit affords me the ability to...

2. **Use the answers above to create more specific goals.**

    I am healthy and fit, so I am able to *remain energized all day and perform at my best.*
    I am healthy and fit, so I would like to *learn how to snow ski.*
    Being healthy and fit affords me the ability to *hike with my kids.*

3. **Build your gratitude and affirmations.**

    I am so grateful that I am healthy, fit, and *have the energy all day to perform my best.*

I am so grateful that I am healthy, fit, and *can learn how to ski.*
I am so grateful that I am healthy and fit so *I can go on hikes with my kids.*

4. Create your list of what you will need.

To have amazing energy all day, I need *to eat healthy food that gives me energy.*
To become a snow skier, I need *to strengthen my legs and increase my stamina.*
To hike with my kids, I need *to be in great cardiovascular condition.*

5. Ask yourself specific questions to help you achieve your goal.

- What healthy foods provide energy?
- What exercises will strengthen my legs?
- What will help me increase my stamina?
- How should I work on my cardiovascular health?
- Who can help me learn how to ski?

To assure your success in reaching a goal, you need to do some soul searching. If your goal is not heartfelt but falls into a "should do" or "ought to do" category, this will impede your progress. Find a goal your heart is truly set on. Also, if your goal is too big to realistically reach, you will set yourself up for failure. So don't set out to become a famous pop singer if you're tone deaf.

When you break down the process of reaching your health goal, you create your map for getting there. You can work through as many "I am healthy and fit" statements as you like in order to get more clarity on what you need to do to reach your goal successfully. When you're satisfied with your statements, pick three from your list to focus on.

Just remember, your attitude will determine how much you can do, and your gratitude will be the momentum behind your ability to do it. Don't underestimate the power of gratitude in your life. It truly works miracles. So keep journaling what you are grateful for and review your list daily.

The Best Times to Review Your Gratitude List
Before your feet hit the ground in the morning. It sets the tone for your entire day.
When you are struggling with an issue. Your list will give you a feeling of support.
When you are feeling overwhelmed. Your list is a powerful reminder to give up the fear.
Before you eat. It is the state of mind/body that is optimal for your cells to actually receive nutrients and digest them properly.
When you exercise. Your body hears your appreciation and will perform and respond better.

Weekly Commitment

Your Activity

- **Dream, Joy, Gratitude, and Affirmation Lists**
  - What did you learn from creating your lists?
  - Did you notice any patterns?
  - How did your lists make you feel?
  - What have you learned about yourself from your lists?

- **Goals and Tools**
  - Pick a new goal and follow the process that was laid out above.
  - Organize your lists and work to achieve your new goal.
  - There is no limit to how many times you can do this exercise.

- **Gratitude**
  - Create a daily gratitude practice at an optimal time each day. Pick three things each day that you are grateful for.

Sign a weekly commitment to your goals that keeps you accountable.
- BSE – Body Status Exam – Check in with how your body is feeling.
- MSE – Mental Status Exam – Check in with what you are thinking.

> **Your Accountability:** Connect with your accountability partner to exchange lists.

Your Journal

Continue to write in your journal 10 minutes a day. Include your goals in your journal and your lists to reach them. Leave enough space to add more to them later. Spend 5 minutes reviewing your entry. If you've left out anything, include it. Review the work you've done in your L2F90 Chronicles.

Your Thoughts and Notes:

Lost to Found in 90 Days: Chapter 10

Chapter 11:
Your Spirituality and Meditation

Rachel's Journey

At this point in the program you've probably surmised that my spiritual path is an important part of my life. Attending church is a powerful part of my week and so it may come as a surprise to you that I come from a Jewish background. My mother and father raised us with a belief in God but we were not particularly religious.

I grew up in one of two non-Christian families in my hometown. Everyone else who I knew was Christian. We celebrated all of the Jewish high holidays (Passover, Hanukkah, etc.). We also celebrated Christmas, which was more like wonderful family time with the added benefit of great food. We said grace at dinner but I never went to Hebrew school to study our faith. We also never really got into any deep, family discussions about God. I just knew that I believed in God, and it gave me great comfort to think that there was someone watching out for me who was far bigger than I was.

Too Close for Comfort

I actually remember the first time that I started praying. A young girl named Polly Klaas was kidnapped from her home. The fact that this happened while her parents were home really frightened me. This took place in a small town that was two hours away from my home. I was 9 years old at the time, and this made a huge and lasting impression on me. This was the reason I started to pray. I remember praying to God to keep me safe. At the end of my prayers I would add, "...and Jesus, if you do exist, you can help too."

I kept praying all the way through college. It gave me comfort. I realized I had a good relationship with God. I knew I could count on Him when I needed Him. He was always there and waiting to assist in any way I needed. When I was having a hard time in my marriage, I would pray to God for guidance. I figured He didn't want me to get divorced. When things got harder, and it looked like that was the direction I was headed, I would ask for forgiveness and the strength to forgive myself.

At that time, I found myself asking God to love me. I also asked God to show me how to love myself. I felt so lost. One of the things I did to manage my pain was to go on daily hikes. It was always in nature that I experienced my deepest connection to God. It's hard to express in words but I became aware that I was standing in His creation in the midst of nature. Those moments held me together.

The Amazing Mrs. Dizon

Around that time, an amazing woman came into my life named Anita Dizon. I met her during one of my company's business functions. She was my very first business coach. My partner Matt and I began to meet with her once a week to go over our business goals. She was inspiring and contributed so much to our growth.

There was one week when Matt couldn't make it to our session. I was having a particularly hard time at home but I didn't share this with anyone – especially my work associates. I walked into Anita's office for our meeting and she could tell immediately that something was wrong. I remember her asking if I was okay. In spite of the fact that I reassured her that I was fine, my eyes began to well up with tears. She asked me again, this time more directly, "What's wrong Darling?" Her motherly instincts would not let me get away with this. God is full of surprises...

apparently it was time for me to share what I was going through!

Finally I admitted that while I had this amazingly positive work environment, I had the exact opposite at home. I shared with her how this was taking a toll on my life. Anita pushed the business talk aside, and I spent the entire hour opening up about my personal life. A huge weight was lifted. She told me that in order for me to be the most productive version of myself at work, I needed to work on the personal side of me as well. Anita had studied Psychology in school and was very active in her church. From this point on, she started to work with me once a week as my life coach. It was fundamentally important for me to act with integrity regarding my marriage. Having a new life coach that supported this 100% was a gift from God. With Anita's support I would make sure my side of the table was clean.

Sermons and Mimosas

During the months that followed, Anita and I became very good friends. Now, years later, she is more like family. When I came to Anita and told her that I was filing for separation but was having a hard time with my decision, she invited me to go to a program her church sponsored called, "Divorce Care." It was a 13-week divorce recovery group. While I was open to the concept of the 13-week program, I politely declined, informing her that I was Jewish. She told me that it didn't matter and I would be welcomed there. Reluctantly, I went.

A few weeks into this program, she invited me to go to church with her for a Sunday sermon. I reminded her again, "Anita...I'm a Jew." And again, she reminded me that all were welcome! She also mentioned that we could go for brunch and mimosas afterward. Needless to say, I went!

I'll never forget walking into church for the first time. This was not your little, quaint New England-style church you picture on Christmas greeting cards. This church is a super-sized mega-experience with a huge membership in Granite Bay, CA. I had absolutely no idea that a church could be so all encompassing! It had an enormous campus and boasted a highly professional, audiovisual department. This was church on steroids! In addition, everyone was very welcoming to me.

There were little booths set up everywhere and I felt quite at home. My company has huge annual events that have a similar flare. I was amazed by how welcomed and comfortable I felt. One of the first things my eyes landed on when I entered the building were coffee stations... everywhere! Again, that worked for me!

Music Is My Medicine

As I walked into the actual sanctuary, I was handed a pen and a pamphlet for that day's sermon. All of a sudden my heart stopped. WHAT was that music? I was honestly listening to the most beautiful music I had ever heard in my life. To share with you, I have a trained ear and a strong musical background. In fact, my first college major was Music before I changed it to Business. Music and singing held a serious place in my heart and I was amazed by the quality of music that was beaming from inside.

Walking into church that very first time, I found myself overcome with emotion. I remember thinking, "They sing here!" And as I mentioned above, this wasn't a small production. The musicians were seriously talented and the church's sound system rivaled top music venues that seat thousands. The music went on for about 15 minutes. I was so overcome that I started to cry. Clearly music was my medicine!

Pastor Curt

When the pastor came up, he wasn't wearing the black and white uniform that you see in movies. He was wearing jeans, Sperry topsiders, and a polo shirt. He introduced himself as "Pastor Curt." I was so confused! He was just a normal guy! Now he did talk about Jesus, the thing I was most nervous about, but I managed to play it cool. You see, in my faith, I had been taught that Jesus was a spiritual teacher, not God's son. I felt guilty even being there.

At the end of the service they asked the question, "Do you accept Jesus Christ as your savior?" I stuck my hands in my pockets! In spite of this, I have to say that my first church experience was pretty positive. As I walked out, everyone thanked me for coming and there were tons of people smiling and chatting outside. It felt pretty good. These were really nice people.

My journey to church, in brief, looked like this: On July 14, 2013, I stepped into a church for the first time. I ended up returning there every Sunday with Anita. Initially, I went just for the music. About six months in, I started to listen to the message. About a year in, I started to receive the message.

A Child of God

Finally, on December 1, 2014, I raised my hand. I had internalized the message. I was a child of God and felt so proud and honored to be His, *and* to accept the Lord as my savior.

My 90 day journey brought me even closer to God. I decided to take a huge leap of faith. I had always prayed to God out of need. During my 90 days, I committed to talking to God daily. However, I was going to hand over my needs and challenges to Him and simply *trust His plan* for me. It's one thing to believe in God or a Higher

Power… it's quite another to *let go* and *know* you'll be taken care of!

I wound up writing a simple yet powerful prayer and read it everyday. In this prayer I told God that I was giving Him full power over my life, and that I trusted His plan for me. I started out by reading it aloud every night before bedtime. I then did something that turned out to have an amazing impact. I recorded myself saying my prayer aloud. Then I set it as my morning alarm. Talk about a powerful way to wake up! Hearing myself allow God to take care of *everything* in my life, every time I woke up actually cemented my faith in God's plan for me.

By the end of my 90 days, I felt a connection to God that was stronger than I had ever experienced. I gained a new sense of freedom and ease. I knew God had my back and that His plan for me would naturally be best. And then it happened (organically I might add); I gave up the chronic stress I felt about meeting the perfect guy who would "complete me." I revised my prayer with a special addendum. I asked God to pick out "Mr. Right" for me and present him in His time – *not* mine! I cannot tell you how much better it felt taking that off my plate! In reality, I had no control over this anyway, so why worry about it? My dating life was now in the perfect hands!

Rachel's Nightly Prayer

Heavenly Father,

I just want to thank You for this wonderful life I have,
and the amazing people You have placed in it.

I thank You for the health you give me, my family, and friends.
I thank You for all the blessings you give.

One thing lays heavy on my heart and I need You, God.
I would like to ask for Your help in finding the right man for me,
and trusting You with the timing. You know who he is.
You know what I need. You know who would be the best
person by my side to do Your will here on earth.

I have a bad history picking men, and I'm giving it up to You.
I can no longer live this life leading it on my own.
I need You to choose my path, and be in charge of
who should join me on my journey.

You know me better than I know me. I trust in You, Father,
with everything I have. You know my wants, and my wish,
but most of all I aim to please You. Please place the right people

*in my life and close the door of the wrong people.
I am honored to be a child of Yours, and live
each day to make You proud.*

*Thank you again, Father, for everything.
Each and everyday, I put my trust, and whole heart in You.*

Amen

Good morning! This is God. I'll be handling ALL your problems today, so relax and have a nice day!

God is the way I find my personal strength and inner peace. For me, going to church every Sunday and saying my special prayer grounds me. It also puts me in the right mindset for the week ahead. I've found this to be indispensable. However, this doesn't mean you have to go out and find God or Jesus in your life if you aren't inclined. What is important is that you find out what it is that gives you peace and a sense of well-being. If yoga or running in the mountains gives you strength and grounds you, good for you! Just make sure to incorporate this into your 90 day journey and make it a lifelong habit. We all need to find our solace in this crazy world we live in!

Meditation

Monks and Hippies

Now let's talk about the value of meditation. If you pay close attention, you'll realize that your mind is ceaselessly generating thoughts, and these thoughts generate a host of emotions. So, we are truly never at rest unless we're in deep sleep. When I first heard about meditation -- the practice of quieting your mind – I thought this was something that only monks and hippies did.

The more I read and learned, the more I realized that some of the most successful people in the business world practice meditation and credit it for their mental clarity and high level of success. I figured I was changing so many other things in my life, why not have an open mind and give it a whirl.

In the beginning this was *really* hard for me. My life is fast-paced and my mind is on overdrive to keep up with it. Quieting my mind was quite the feat! I would try to close my eyes and breathe deeply but a moment later I found myself thinking about a client I needed to call or an email I forgot to write. This wasn't going smoothly. I was nervous… even insecure about meditating. I like being good at what I do!

Oprah's Guru

I decided that I needed to do a little more research. I went online and found my way to Dr. Deepak Chopra. He had Oprah's seal of approval, so I figured he would work for me. I went online and found one of his guided meditations. I had never tried this before but I was determined.

I'm happy to report that this did the trick. I now had a map to follow. I was asked to sit in a comfortable position and to quiet my mind. While I started out pretty skeptical, over the next 20 minutes, I breathed deeper, felt calmer, and my thoughts slowed down… way down! The mind follows your breath. Who knew? As I slowed down my breathing to a deep, rhythmic pace, the frenetic speed of my thoughts also slowed down.

I was now more relaxed than I had been in months! My high speed brain finally had its glorious moment to rest and replenish itself. And this is exactly how and why solutions can come from quieting your mind. It gives your brain a chance to rest, relax and reboot. In the process, it can come up with some amazingly creative and spontaneous solutions to your life's biggest challenges.

The guided meditation technique really worked wonders for me and I'm sure it will for you too. The nervousness I had previously felt now vanished. Since my thoughts were never ending, I was instructed to simply observe the thoughts and let them go. Eventually my mind would stop hurling them at me. It was amazingly simple and it worked. After a while of doing this, I was able to recreate these quiet moments in nature. I'd hike to a beautiful place and then sit calmly, closing my eyes and breathing deeply. It helped if I inhaled through my nose and exhaled through my mouth. I would do this breath work over and over again until my mind went silent and I found my inner calm. This was a brave new me!

Nina's Knowledge: Spirituality

I have a favorite quote:

You never hear the answers if you don't stop talking. A quiet mind equals clarity.

Spirituality

On this 90 day journey, you've been focusing on your physical, emotional and mental self. You've been getting to know yourself on a deeper level. To go even deeper requires exploring your spiritual self. Having a connection to something beyond the physical world can provide you with the strength, comfort, solutions, and healing you need in order to face, and overcome, your deepest challenges.

Few of us take the time to get quiet and tap into the immensely loving energy that causes our heart to beat and our lungs to pull air. But what is that energy and how can we utilize it in our lives? This is territory that requires curiosity, faith, and practice. Don't worry if this doesn't come naturally. Everyone can learn to connect to the source that guides his or her life.

Physical Connection

When I walk around in the world, I observe the majority of people focusing their energy into particular areas of their bodies. For example, if people are extremely busy, tense, and concentrating, they will hold the majority of their energy in their head. This can lead to severe headaches. If people are troubled emotionally, they tend to hold most of their energy in their chest/heart. If this occurs consistently, this can put a tremendous strain on the heart and cause problems down the road. If people are feeling stressed and burdened by tremendous responsibilities, their energy will concentrate in their shoulders and back. They are literally "carrying" an energetic burden and their shoulders and back will suffer.

These are the most common areas that I notice people holding their energy. Having worked with numerous clients for over two decades now, I actually see and feel where their energy is concentrated and blocked. This empathic response requires paying attention on a deep level. We all have this ability. Reading people's bodies and energy fields helps me to understand more about what they are going through and how I can help them.

Working on the areas that you find you are holding most of your energy will allow you to have emotional releases and physical healing. You can do this through healing modalities, yoga, and a host of other techniques. In addition, physical exercise is one of the most effective means for bringing your body back into balance because it forces your energy to circulate. It also helps you release and reduce stress. Exercise enables you to redistribute your energy throughout your entire body.

When you exercise it is akin to switching on the main circuit breaker. Electricity flows freely to all areas of the body like it would in a house. When our bodies are in physical balance we are more connected to our heart, our loved ones, and our Source. And this creates a sense of well being.

Your Physical Layout
- Do you know where you hold or block your energy?
- Do you notice specific times that your energy seems to be in those areas?
- What does it feel like in the areas you are holding energy (hot, cold, pins and needles, tight, pain, etc.)?
- Look at yourself in the mirror. Take 10 deep breaths. Do you notice any changes in your body as you are breathing?
- Are you surprised about any of your answers to the above?
- Are you able to use your breath to redistribute your energy throughout your entire body?
- Do you notice anything else?

Meditation

Meditation allows you the opportunity to connect to your heart and soul. At the same time, your mind gets the rare opportunity to rest. The reward for this is outstanding. Your brain will become energized and you will feel calmly active and actively calm. Most meditation practices focus on clearing the mind by drawing your attention to your breath. Other techniques will use visualization exercises to bring you to a deep state of relaxation and a heightened state of awareness. While the above may seem simple, these techniques require a disciplined practice in order to reap their benefits. It is called a meditation practice because you don't immediately become an expert, you will need to practice, so be patient.

Sit in a comfortable place. Close your eyes and focus on your breath. Just listen to and watch your breath go in and out for five minutes. If you fall asleep, don't worry. Try it again later.

A hint: As you begin your practice, don't try to force your thoughts to stop. This has a way of increasing their flow. I like to encourage people to simply let their thoughts pass by without giving them full attention. Visualize the tickers that run across the bottom of your television screen and you'll get the idea. When a thought arises, just look for the next pause between your thoughts. It is easier to focus on what you want, so focus on the quiet space between your thoughts and increasingly this space will grow in length.

Find a New Direction: Rhythm

Exercise 1: A Quiet Mind

A quiet mind will allow you to connect to your body and feel its rhythm.

1. Sit with your feet on the floor.
   - Find a comfortable position.
   - Focus on your body.

2. Are there any areas that are calling your attention?
   - Respond to your body by stretching the areas that may be tight and painful. Change position if this is what your body wants. The important thing is to respond to what your body is telling you.
   - When you are settled, focus on your breathing.
   - Allow your ribcage to expand wide rather than up. You want to breathe deeply into your diaphragm. Avoid shallow chest breathing.

3. Prepare to connect with your body.
   - Feel your feet touching the floor.
   - Feel your legs touching the chair.
   - Feel your weight in the chair.
   - Feel your breath.
   - Feel your neck elongating.
   - Feel your head floating on top of your spine.
   - Breathe into your entire body.

4. Continue to feel your breath in your entire body.

This simple exercise will get you out of your head and present in your body. Once you've practiced this enough and feel connected to your body, you may also feel a connection with others and the world at large. Doing this exercise for as little as two minutes can create a palpable shift in your body.

Pause for Reflection
What did you notice when you did this exercise?
How did it change your mental and physical state?
Did you notice a connection to the people or environment around you?

Exercise 2: Moments of Centeredness

When you commit to a daily meditation practice, you're essentially committing yourself to a powerful vehicle that can change your life. Meditation increases your ability to perform. It connects you to your source. It makes you more resistant to stress and provides you with a higher level of thinking.

You'll find your level of patience will increase while your stress level decreases. Ultimately you will experience higher levels of success and a feeling of empowerment.

Meditate for three straight days. Note what works for you and what doesn't.

Exercise 3: Mini Quiet Times - 10 Deep Breaths

If for any reason you find yourself resisting meditation, start with 10 deep breaths. Include your 10 deep breaths in your daily calendar and use your phone or watch to remind you to take them. Use this technique as often as possible.

For instance, take 10 deep breaths while you're waiting for someone to answer the phone. Take 10 deep breaths when you're in traffic. Do them while you type an email. It's amazing how powerful this simple technique is. It can lower your blood pressure, increase your circulation, relax your muscles, quiet a headache, and reset many other body functions. It can also halt negative thought patterns and calm you down.

Practice this technique now.

Pause for Reflection
Do you notice any physical changes?
What kind of changes in your thoughts, mood, and/or body did you experience?

Reflection: Getting Information

Quieting your mind brings clarity. It will ground and center you. You'll have an increased sense of awareness. You will literally see, hear, and feel things differently. It is very much like having blinders removed. You'll have the ability to capture more information around you. You'll be able to perceive things on a deeper level and sense divine/intuitive guidance. Life actually gets easier when you are in this state. You're in "the zone"!

Weekly Commitment

Your Activity

- Physical Connection
  - How do you feel when you think about your body, mind, and spiritual connection?
  - What do you notice when you're connecting on a deeper level to your body, mind and spirit?
  - Do you have areas that have more going on or need more attention?
  - Can you circulate your energy throughout your body?

- Meditation
  - Choose a meditation practice (a guided technique is fine).
  - Do your practice every day this week at the same time.

- Rhythm
  - Listen to and feel your body's rhythm.
  - What does it feel like?
  - When do you feel it?

- Moments of Centeredness and Mini Quiet Time
  - Pick a moment once a day to take 10 deep breaths.

- Information
  - Write down the thoughts and observations that come to you after your meditation practice.

Your Accountability: Connect with your accountability partner and share your meditation practice and experience.

Your Journal

Use 5 minutes in your schedule to review your past entries and responses to the questions you have answered in your L2F90 Chronicles. Then write in your journal for 10 minutes each day.

Goal Review:

- Journal your experience with your meditation exercises.
- Sign a weekly commitment to your goals that keeps you accountable.
- BSE – Body Status Exam – Check in with how your body is feeling.
- MSE – Mental Status Exam – Check in with what you are thinking.

Your Thoughts and Notes:

Lost to found in 90 Days: Chapter 11

Chapter 12:
Your Quiet Time and Self-Love

Rachel's Journey

When I found myself entering the last week of my 90 day challenge, I made some amazing observations. The first was that I truly had found myself along the way. This was such a departure from the lost me that had started this program. I remember thinking, "Hey, something has really shifted. People are asking me what I'm doing differently and they keep telling me I'm glowing." The only thing my work associates knew was that I had stopped drinking. I hadn't shared my journey with them but they sure noticed a difference.

This was my astonishing mental inventory during the last week of my journey:

"I am now 32 pounds lighter and I feel good about myself. I not only look better. I feel better! I wake every morning to my prayer. I'm drinking water, working out, and journaling about what I'm grateful for. I'm eating clean whole foods and my body is reflecting this. The care I'm showing my body has affected my entire life. I'm more productive and highly energized. My numbers are up at the office and my partner is thrilled over our heightened success and my "laser focus." I'm always in a great mood. I feel light, I feel connected to God, and I'm closer with my friends than ever before. I know this is because of my commitment to BEING PRESENT. I can't believe how hyper-aware I've become about my environment. I surround myself with like-minded individuals who are goal driven, want big lives, and love with their whole hearts."

My MSE

I started to read my past journal entries for the heck of it. I could see how I had changed and this really thrilled me. The observations below came from my MSE:

"The way I speak to myself has changed. I am kinder to myself. I am more forgiving. I am stronger and feel centered. I can't quite put my finger on it but I know that something significant has shifted inside me. I feel like a better version of myself."

I feel like a better version of myself.

90 Days to Success

I think it was about day 88 when I was driving to visit my parents. My windows were down and I was singing my heart out to a song on the radio. I glanced to my right and I saw a fruit stand. I love fresh fruit, as does my family, so I stopped to bring some home. I walked up to the fruit stand packed with California's finest. I decided on peaches and cherries. This fruit stand is located in a beautiful area surrounded by orchards. I remember taking a peach out of the bag and walking toward a row of fruit trees. I inhaled deeply and savored the smell of that sweet, juicy peach.

I felt an overwhelming sense of calm and gratitude. I was so buoyant and alive. In this magical moment, I realized the power of self-love and forgiveness. No longer plagued by the guilt of my divorce, I was physically, mentally, emotionally, and spiritually a thousand times lighter and brighter! I was no longer tied down by the weight of self-criticism. I finally realized that I deserved to move forward, and I was soaring.

When I realized that I had stopped looking to the external world to fill me up, I was astonished. In that precious moment, I was entirely filled with love, and this love came from taking care of myself in a way I had never done before.

My beautiful 90 day experiment allowed me the inner quietude to find clarity, happiness, self-acceptance and ultimately, peace. I had found the joy I had been searching for and it wasn't in a cocktail, dessert, or "Mr. Right." It was inside of me. I couldn't help but love myself!

Make Your "Once Upon a Time" Happen

Before my program, I had this fairy tale. I thought that the love I was searching for would come from another person – specifically my "perfect" mate. I just had to find him! I never expected to find the kind of love I was searching for from within. I had always heard that you couldn't love another person until you loved yourself. I finally understood what this meant. How can you love another person if you can't accept yourself and don't truly know who you are, what you want, and what you deserve? You have to know your own heart first. You have to know your needs and what makes you happy and sad. You need clarity on who you want to become and where you want to go.

It really comes down to this: If you never had to care about what anyone else thought... If you never had to worry about your next paycheck ... If it didn't matter how much you weighed or how you looked... What would your life look like? What would it be like to live for you? Don't you deserve this? We live in a beautiful world and you have an opportunity to live a beautiful life. Now it's up to you to go after it!

When I started my 90 day journey, I was lost and feeling slightly broken. I had no idea why people raved about their 30s. I ended my 90th day with a whole new outlook. I am confident in who I am and what I want out of life. I am clear on the kind of partnership I want in the future. I treat everyone with care and enjoy genuine connections because I am present with them. I have faith in God's plan for me and it makes me smile.

*I am confident in who I am and
what I want out of life.*

The Power of Your Positive Mind

When I look back, I am amazed by the results of my 90 day journey. My real estate team ended the year with $36 million in sales which landed us in Wall Street Journal's Top 1,000 Real Estate Agents in the country! My leadership skills have evolved because I'm able to lead by example. I now teach my team how to schedule their mornings for success. I talk to my team about positive mindsets. And I'm happy to report that I'm back in size 4 clothing!

This 90 day program has truly transformed my life. I not only like myself, I like who I am becoming! This is a continuing journey and I now get the opportunity to pick two new distractions for my next 90 days! Self-improvement is a lifelong adventure! There will always be people I can learn from. I am committed to being a student of LIFE!

Guiding you on your transformational journey is a passion of mine. Get ready to be amazed by what you are capable of. I can't wait to watch you develop into the person you have always longed to be!

Nina's Knowledge:
Your Quiet Time and Self-Love

Your Lost to Found journey has been an opportunity to create a positive, healthy relationship with yourself. Twelve weeks ago you had a closet full of old beliefs, patterns, and feelings. These limited your life experiences in multiple ways. Successes are built upon a positive mindset. Your healthy body and commitment to take the actions required to meet your goals are all a product of your powerful mind. During your 90 day journey, you cleaned your closet and let go of the things that weren't supporting your overall well-being. This will continue to sustain you throughout your life.

It's time to quiet your mind and review your journey. Schedule uninterrupted time to examine your victories, challenges, and new level of empowerment. You've made changes from the inside out and your foundation is strong. You have developed new tools for reaching your goals. Your new tools will give you positive outcomes!

Review the work you've done over the past 90 days. Read through your responses to all of the questions. They will show you where you started and where you ended up. You are on a new path!

Read your journal. Often we forget some of the details that altered the course of our life. Your journal holds a record of things you may have forgotten. This will keep you motivated and inspired to continue to grow on the new path you've taken. Pay particular attention to the new realizations you've gained. Remember, your journey isn't over. It's just beginning. You are now prepared to take charge of your life and fulfill your dreams.

Your Gratitude List

There are so many things for which to be grateful. Take the time to acknowledge all that supports your well-being. Recognize the many ways you have changed and the new path you're on. This will empower you to continue to succeed. Gratitude rewards you with heartfelt energy that fuels future success.

Your Self-Acknowledgment

You've achieved much on your 90 day journey. Your commitment to doing things differently and making positive changes has transformed your life. Make a list of what you've done well and how you've shined. Include everything that you're proud of.

Take a moment to honor your hard work and successes. You've done an outstanding job!

Acknowledgment from Others

Sometimes the best way to see yourself is through the eyes of your inner circle. Ask your accountability partner, friends, family members, co-workers and Lost to Found Community how you have changed. Include their observations and praise in your journal so you can see how far you've come. You've come a long way!

Your New Found Direction

You have everything you need to make your life wonderful and it all comes from within. Your new path will continue to make you the best version of yourself. Your physical, mental, emotional and spiritual health will support your goals and help you fulfill your dreams. Embrace the newly transformed you!

Weekly Commitment

Your Activity

What are you grateful for regarding your 90 day journey? Here are some sentences to get you started acknowledging your accomplishments and expressing your gratitude:

- I am so proud and thankful that I...
- I did a great job_____and am so grateful because...
- I am so thankful that I now believe I can…
- I am so thankful that my new self-confidence allows me to…

Fill in what you are grateful for in the chart below.

Gratitude List
1.
2.
3.
4.
5.
6.

Ask 5-10 people in your inner circle to tell you something positive they have noticed about you on your journey. Record who gave you what kudos.

Person	Kudos

Your Accountability: Connect with your accountability partner to give them gratitude and praise for the crucial role they played on your journey. Share three things he/she did for you that you appreciate. In addition, share three of their strengths that you admire.

Your Journal

Include your final Body Status Exam - scan your body, head to toe, and check in with how your body is feeling.

Include your final Mental Status Exam - scan your mind/thoughts, and check in with what you are thinking and feeling.

While your 90 day challenge is now complete, YOUR journey is just getting started. Keep your Lost 2 Found Chronicles and your journal for reference. They can continue to inspire you for years. Know that you can surprise yourself by remaining committed to your ongoing growth and well-being. Make sure to stay in touch and let us know how your journey evolves. We have complete faith that your efforts will be rewarded. And remember, your Lost to Found Community is here to support you!

Your Thoughts and Notes:

Lost to Found in 90 Days: Chapter 12

Lost to Found in 90 Days: Chapter 12

Lost to Found in 90 Days: Chapter 12

Lost to Found in 90 Days: Chapter 12

Final Note to Reader

Your potential is unlimited when you choose to challenge yourself. Completing this 90 day journey with you has been a privilege. We are so proud of you!

Congratulations on moving from Lost to Found!

Make sure to share your continued accomplishments with us on social media. Your L2F90 Family is always here for you!

#L2F90

now...

Take a deep breath and know that **YOU** are all you need to be fulfilled!

With great faith in your future,

Made in the USA
San Bernardino, CA
07 January 2016